PATRICIA BERRY

JUNG'S EARLY PSYCHIATRIC WRITING

The Emergence of a Psychopoetics

SPRING PUBLICATIONS
THOMPSON, CONN.

Published by Spring Publications
Thompson, Conn.
www.springpublications.com

First edition 2023 (1.3)

Originally submitted in 1983 to the Graduate Faculty of the University of Dallas in partial fulfillment of the requirements for the degree of Doctor of Philosophy in Psychology in the Institute of Philosophic Studies.

ISBN: 978-0-88214-139-8

Library of Congress Control Number: 2023936521

CONTENTS

INTRODUCTION

This book is concerned with the making of psychotherapeutic ideas and the way in which these ideas issue into the practices of psychological interpretation and psychological therapy. Its focus is the depth psychology of C.G. Jung with particular reference to his early psychiatric work. Jung's early work has received little attention, since it is generally assumed that these clinical writings (composed between 1902 and 1911), represent Jung before he was Jung—that is, before his ideas had cohered into a distinct and characteristic approach within depth psychology.

To a certain extent this attitude is correct, since during this period Jung of course did not know that his ideas would eventually coalesce into a distinct kind of depth psychology termed "Jungian," and so he did not present them as foundational. But many of these ideas were implicit already in his early work, influencing his observations, his choice of topics, and his manners of treatment. An advantage in looking to this period before Jung had elaborated his psychology is that we can witness his thinking in its formation, viewing its complexities as representative of psychological thinking in general, yet also particular to his personal psychology.

This psychological complexity appears as two distinct attitudes in various combinations with various effects throughout Jung's work. One attitude is scientific, concerned with the systematization of facts into structures of comprehensive meaning. The other is aesthetic, given to activities of fantasy and imagination—painting, building, sculpturing, "speaking" with imaginary figures. In these aesthetic activities Jung engages with imaginal phenomena in concrete particular immediacy.

The task of this dissertation is twofold. One is to trace Jung's two attitudes, which appear in his personal psychology as well as in his theoretical ideas and methods of interpretation. The second is to imagine a psychological approach based explicitly on making. The two are related in that by tracing Jung's methods in terms of their making, with an eye to the kinds of constructions he uses and for what reasons, we shall gather from his psychology the basis for our approach. Our underlying assumption is that depth psychology, despite its scientific claims, is also a *psychopoiesis*.[1]

In coining the term *psychopoiesis*, we borrow from the original Greek, where poiesis refers to making generally without limiting it to productions of a literary kind. The modern associations with art evoked by this word are helpful for our purposes in that they color psychology as an artful rather than a scientific or objective discipline. So, too, with the word "making," which we shall use synonymously with poiesis to refer to the psychological activity of forming and formation.

Precedents for this broad sense of art appear in Nietzsche's concept of art, which, according to Heidegger's reading, "is obviously extended to every ability to bring forth and to everything that is essentially brought forth"[2] and to the sense implied by Jacques Maritain when he says. that "by art [he means] the creative or producing, work-making activity of the human mind."[3]

---

1. The term originated with David L. Miller, "Mythopoiesis, Psychopoiesis, Theopoiesis: The Poetics of Meaning," Panarion Conference, Los Angeles, August 1976.

2. Martin Heidegger, *Nietzsche: The Will Power as Art*, 2 vols., translated by David Farrell Krell (New York: Harper & Row, 1979), 1: 71.

3. Jacques Maritain, *Creative Intuition in Art and Poetry* (Princeton, N.J.: Princeton University Press, 1977 [1953]), 3.

Until the nineteenth century this extended connotation of the word art was common usage.[4]

Aesthetic, another word I employ, refers to the Greek *aisthesis* in its original meaning "of the senses" or "pertaining to perception."[5] This usage is distinct from those that characterize the aesthetic more specifically as having to do with beauty. In my use aesthetic will refer to a sensateness or sensuousness as it is experienced through the imagination, as if it were sensate, not literally derivative of the senses but imaginatively sensuous and concrete.

I shall also be drawing upon Jung's notion of image. Image is a way of speaking of the contexts within which making takes place. In Jung's usage it is a paradoxical notion, in that image refers to both the condition for and the result of fantasy activity; it is both a requirement of imaginative work and its object. Because it is one of the few terms, however, that Jung provides which refers explicitly to an imaginal, poetic realm of psychic events, I have opted to retain it, and to separate out its ambiguities as they occur.

Since the purpose of this undertaking is to explore psychopoiesis I shall not be guided by Jung's statements of what he is about or take his systematic structures literally as immovable givens. I shall be concerned more with what Jung does than with what he says about what he does, and with the way his structures work, interrelate, sometimes cancel each other out within the contexts of his particular psychiatric activities. Since his psychological ideation, interpretation, and therapeutic treatment issue from a basis in psychological making, these makings will be seen as more or less effective constructions in their rendering of psychological processes.

---

4. Heidegger, *Nietzsche*, 1: 71.
5. *Oxford English Dictionary*, 1971 ed., s.v. "aesthetic," "poetic."

My attitude in regard to these makings shall be pragmatic in that any notions concerning what is "reality" or what is "true" or even what are the essential "goals" and "needs" of human life shall be, for the sake of our primary concern with making, bracketed. From a position that regards making as primary, assertions regarding values or goals, truth or reality, become contextual, i.e., relevant only where they inhere in makings.

My approach will also be pragmatic in that it will emphasize, as does William James, the "distinctively concrete, the individual, the particular, and effective, as opposed to the abstract, general and inert."[6] Because of my bias in this regard, the dissertation intends not to develop new abstract structures but to view any and all structures in terms of their usefulness for making.

There is, however, an informing perspective for this making. This perspective is rooted in Jung. It involves what he calls *esse in anima* (being in anima). Attitudes that emerge from this grounding—Jung's regard for multiplicity, his emphasis on particularity and on the imaginal nature of psychic reality, and his focus upon the intentionality of autonomous psychic factors—such as complexes, symptoms, and all else that appears ununderstandable from a rationally systematic point of view—inform this psychopoetic perspective.

A word on structure. My inquiry proceeds in a circular manner. Many of the points touched upon in earlier chapters reappear in later chapters as well. Given the shifting, insubstantial nature of the anima (as shall be explained in Chapter One) whose movements underlie Jung's ideation—this organization and its repetitions are unavoidable. The areas of focus comprising each of the chapters of our inquiry—from Jung's personal breakdown in the

---

6. William James, *The Meaning of Truth* (Cambridge, Mass. and London: Harvard University Press, 1975), 113.

first chapter to the final chapters involving psychopathology and its treatment—are intercontingent. Hence the work may best be imagined a layering, each layer superimposed on the others.

Since psychopathology is a theme throughout the dissertation, and necessary to its aesthetic, the final chapter addresses the question of treatment directly, offering points of consideration for psychotherapeutic practice. These offerings deliberately eschew premature precision. They intend to point toward areas of practical consideration in a spirit of opening rather than solving. Given our thesis of psychological making, there is no guarantee that principles abstracted from any particular contexts will work in any particular one. The extent to which a psychological making works depends finally on characteristics unique to the particular situation of the making.

CHAPTER ONE

The Problem: The Aesthetic Anima

After his *Wandlungen und Symbole der Libido* in 1912 and his final break with Freud, Jung went through a period of uncertainty, even disorientation lasting nearly eight years.[1] During this "creative illness," Jung's psychiatric approach changed.[2] He put aside his theoretical premises and, simply letting his patients speak, opened the analytical situation to whatever might occur.

> My aim became to leave things to chance [*was der Zufall brachte*]. The result was that the patients would spontaneously report their dreams and fantasies to me, and I would merely ask, "What occurs to you in connection with that?" or, "How do you mean that, where does that come from, what do you think about it?" The interpretations seemed to follow of their own accord from the patients' replies and associations. I avoided all theoretical points of view and simply helped the patients to understand the dream-images by themselves, without application of rules and theories.[3]

---

1. C.G. Jung, "Wandlungen und Symbole der Libido. Beiträge zur Entwicklungsgeschichte des Denkens," *Jahrbuch für Psychoanalytische und Psychopathologische Forschungen 3*, no. 1 (1911): 120–227; 4, no. 2 (1912): 162–464. Published in English with the title *Symbols of Transformation* as volume 5 of *The Collected Works of C.G. Jung*, edited and translated by Gerhard Adler and R.F.C. Hull, 20 vols. (Princeton, N.J.: Princeton University Press, 1953–79); hereinafter cited as *CW* followed by the volume and paragraph numbers, unless noted otherwise.

2. Cf. Henri F. Ellenberger, *The Discovery of the Unconscious: The History and Evolution of Dynamic Psychiatry* (London: Allen Lane, 1970), 672.

3. C.G. Jung, *Memories, Dreams, Reflections*, recorded and edited by Aniela Jaffé; translated by Richard and Clara Winston (New York: Vintage

By putting aside his theoretical rules and suppositions Jung accorded the psyche its own coherence.

> Soon I realized that it was right to take the dreams in this way as the basis of interpretation, for that is how dreams are intended. They are the facts from which we must proceed.[4]

To begin with dream as fact is to orient in terms of the psyche's own phenomena. What the psyche produces while the conscious personality is asleep takes priority over conscious constructions, reasonable and objective thought. Reality is no longer defined as necessarily external and public. It obtains as well when the conscious mind is unaware.[5] Dreams are, in other words, phenomenal, primary manifestations from which interpretation takes its bearing. Dreams, rather than deriving from, precede conscious constructions and elaborations.

As Jung accredited the dream full phenomenal status, he found himself without theoretical support. Freud viewed the dream as a derived phenomenon, a substitution;[6] previously Jung had relied on this psychoanalytic understanding of what he was about—or thought he had. In fact, in *Wandlungen und Symbole der Libido* he departed significantly from Freud's reductive method, viewing psychic manifestations as more particular and meaningful in themselves than Freud had maintained. Psychic

---

Books, 1973), 170; hereinafter cited as *MDR*. Published originally in German as *Erinnerungen Träume Gedanken von C. G. Jung* (Zurich and Stuttgart: Rascher Verlag, 1962).

  4. *MDR*, 171.

  5. Jung uses the term "psychic reality" to refer to reality as it is experienced whether its source be an external "fact" or an internal thought. "If I shift my concept of reality on to the plane of the psyche—where alone it is valid—this puts an end to the conflict between mind and matter, spirit and nature, as contradictory explanatory principles" (*CW* 8: 681).

  6. Cf. Sigmund Freud, *On Dreams*, translated by James Strachey (London: Hogarth, 1952), 11.

libido was broader than sexuality.[7] The process of symbol formation was not merely the result of repression and displacement but
was as well the psyche's inherent tendency to develop and transform itself. Culture did not exist to safeguard the psyche from the
lower and more destructive impulses of the id; rather, culture was
an expression of the psyche, not derived or projected from it, but
analogous to it. Jung's canvas was broader, his sense of symbol
and ritual, and his regard for the phenomena of the psyche less
reductive and materialistic than was Freud's.[8]

But at the time to which Jung refers in his autobiography his
ground was tenuous. He had no theoretical formulation to support what he was about, no system to establish his experience
methodologically. Without this support he was disoriented.

> Naturally, the aspects resulting from this method [regard-
> ing the psyche's manifestations as primary] were so multi-
> tudinous that the need for a criterion grew more and more
> pressing—the need...for some initial orientation.[9]

As Jung was experimenting in this open-ended manner with his
patients, he also was engaged in an exploration of his own psyche.
In a search for orientation he went back over the details of his
personal life, his childhood memories and traumas, to see what
"might possibly be the cause" of his present disturbance. Finding

---

7. Sexuality as exemplified in incest is given a broader meaning by Jung.
"It is not incestuous cohabitation that is desired, but rebirth. The effect of
the incest-taboo and of the attempts at canalization is to stimulate the creative imagination, which gradually opens up possible avenues for the self
realization of libido. In this way the libido becomes imperceptibly spiritualized" (CW5: 332).

8. CW5; cf. particularly pars. 194ff., where Jung speaks of libido as
having a general intentionality rather than an intentionality limited to
any one instinct; par. 652, where he distinguishes a psychological from a
physical cosmogony.

9. MDR, 171.

no key in the past, he turned to his more recent activities. *In Wandlungen und Symbole der Libido* "the hero" was the central figure. But to be honest with himself Jung had to admit that the hero was not his own personal myth, nor did Christianity solve the problems—though he had drawn on Christian symbolism in his book. Jung was at "a dead end [*Ich war an eine Grenze gekommen*]."[10]

Around Christmas of 1912 Jung had a dream in which a white bird, a seagull or a dove, descended and turned into a little girl. As a little girl she played with Jung's children and then tenderly put her arms around his neck. Turning back into a dove, she said in a human voice, "Only in the first hours of the night can I transform myself into a human being, while the male dove is busy with the twelve dead." She then flew away, and Jung awoke. Jung pieced through the symbols of the dream, noting that it showed "an unusual activation of the unconscious," but was finally unable to interpret its meaning.[11] Defeated, Jung again vowed simply to submit himself to whatever emerged from the unconscious.

What emerged was the memory of an activity he had engaged in as a child. At age eleven or twelve he had occupied himself building constructions out of blocks, stone, mud, glass. The memory rekindled an excitement.

> "Aha," I said to myself, "there is still life in these things. The small boy [*kleine Junge*] is still and, and, and possesses a creative life which I lack."[12]

A figure spontaneously emerges, a small boy, with a creative life that the ego feels itself lacking. Jung does not regard this figure as

---

10. *MDR*, 166.

11. Ibid. For a discussion of this dream and its implications, see Robert Grinnell, "Reflections on the Archetype of Consciousness: Personality and Psychological Faith," *Spring: An Annual of Archetypal Psychology and Jungian Thought* (1970): 15–39.

12. *MDR*, 173–74.

a personified projection of himself, but rather as a character with its own autonomy and animation.[13] Though the boy is· connected with a memory of Jung's own boyhood, as a figure he is beyond Jung and independent of his adult personality. As an independent and in this sense "impersonal" figure, the child possesses something that Jung himself is lacking. To gain connection with this figure Jung takes up a similar activity.

> I had no choice but to return to it and take up once more that child's life with his childish games. This moment was a turning point in my fate, but I gave in only after endless resistances and with a sense of resignation. For it was a painfully humiliating experience to realize that there was nothing to be done except play childish games.[14]

Jung's return to childhood is by way of an activity with a mimetic relation to a childhood activity. His focus is not on an "event" of his childhood as key to his present difficulties or on an emotion to "abreact" rather his intention is the revitalization of a childhood passion.[15] By approaching this child through action rather than seeking a meaning or an insight about the memory, Jung is placing activity before knowing, making before insight or ideation. This making occurs in an interim place between the present activity with its purpose and the memory of an activity in the past.

Making is a kind of *poiesis*—in this case not with words but concretely through the senses, the handling of mud and stone to

---

13. It is important to remember that Jung regards these figures phenomenally, not as inventions of the conscious subject. "It is not we who personify them; they have a personal nature from the very beginning" (*CW* 13: 62).

14. *MDR*, 168.

15. For a discussion of Jung's concrete play, see Daniel C. Noel, "Veiled Kabir: C.G. Jung's Phallic Self Image," *Spring: An Annual of Archetypal Psychology and Jungian Thought* (1974): 224–42.

form a structure.[16] Thus the activity is also an *aisthesis,* i.e., of the senses. Jung does not speak of the goal of the activity as beauty or truth or wholeness or any other abstraction. The goal is in the service of a psychic process—in this case the experience of the child--which can be served only through an enactment, mimetic in relation to something beyond itself which gives to it the character of a rite or ritual.[17]

> Naturally, I thought about the significance of what I was doing, and asked myself, "Now, really, what are you about? You are building a small town, and doing it as if it were a rite [*Ritus*]!"[18]

The activity is a rite in that there is an echo or second level to it; it is a re-enactment, a doing in the service of something other. Jung continues:

---

16. For "making as kind of poiesis" I draw upon the sense of making emphasized by Robert Creeley. In his discussion of William Carlos Williams' insistence that a poem be *made,* Creeley comments, "the sense of poetry that's evident in Williams' introduction to *The Wedge* when he says, 'When a man makes a poem, *makes* it, mind you,' so that it has 'an intrinsic movement of its own to verify its authenticity'—in other words, so that it is not simply a wish on the part of the writer (or not simply a communication, saying 'I'm telling you this'), but has within it all that it needs to survive in its own statement. This, I feel, is a necessary condition for a poem that's active" (Interview manuscript, 1964: cited by Linda W. Wagner, "'Oh, Pioneers!' One Sense of Creeley's 'Place'" in *Robert Creeley: The Poet's Workshop,* edited by Caroll F. Terrell (Orono: National Poetry Foundation, University of Maine at Orono, 1984), 179.

17. The notion of mimesis used here and throughout derives from Maritain's understanding of poetry as an imitation with nature's way of operating, based on an "intercommunication between the inner being of things and the inner being of the human Self" (Maritain, *Creative Intuition in Art and Poetry,* 3). This idea of imitation reappears in Ananda K. Coomaraswamy's *The Transformation of Nature in Art* (New York: Dover Press, 1956), and in John Cage's *A Year From Monday* (Middletown, Conn.: Wesleyan University Press, 1967); cf. pp. 31, 75.

18. *MDR,* 174.

I had no answer to my question, only the inner certainty that I was on the way to discovering my own myth. For the building game [*Das Bauen*] was only a beginning. It released a stream of fantasies which I later carefully wrote down. This sort of thing has been consistent with me, and at any time in my later life when I came up against a blank wall, I painted a picture or hewed stone. Each such experience proved to be a *rite d'entrée* fort ideas and works that followed hard upon it.[19]

The making activities that Jung here describes are to become basic to his therapeutic practice. Painting, drawing, and shaping in clay are expressions of the active imagination, primary therapeutic practices attesting to an important experiential level of Jung's psychology.

Making as a ritual serves "psychic reality," a reality "other" than the known reality of ego consciousness.[20]

This "other" reality appears as well in Jung's imaginal dialogues with psychic figures, a technique he came to call "active imagination."[21] In the following passage he describes his conversation with one of these "imaginal others."

In my fantasies I held conversations [*Phantasiegespräche*] with him, and he said things which I had not consciously thought. For I observed clearly that it was he who spoke, not I. He said I treated thoughts as if I generated them myself, but in his view thoughts were like animals in the forest, or people in a room, or birds in the air, and added, "If you should see people in a room, you would not think that

---

19. Ibid., 174–75.

20. For Jung's discussions of "psychic reality," see *CW*5: 222; *CW*7: 151, 158; *CW*8: 681, 683, 743, 748; *CW*9.2: 85; *CW*11: 376, 766, 888; *CW*12: 93; *CW* 13: 62, 76n.

21. For a complete listing of Jung's references to active imagination, see R.F.C. Hull, "Bibliographical Notes on Active Imagination in the Works of C.G. Jung," *Spring: An Annual of Archetypal Psychology and Jungian Thought* (1971): 115–20.

you had made those people, or that you were responsible for them." It was he who taught me psychic objectivity, the reality of the psyche. Through him [*Durch die Gespräche mit Philemon*] the distinction was clarified between myself and the object of my thought. He confronted me in an objective manner, and I understood that there is something in me which can say things that I do not know and do not intend, things which may even be directed against me.[22]

Here Jung recognizes psychic reality as "objective," separate from but as real as the ego's reality. Thoughts are not generated by the ego but are alive with their own intentionality, like animals or other people outside the ego's personal domain and responsibility.

That the psyche is objective and impersonal gives to the imagination an autonomy far beyond any personalistic reductions, and even beyond the ego's experience of itself. Psychic figures may contradict the ego's feeling. The imagination is other, and its figures and dynamics autonomous, outside the ego's control. It is up to the ego to make its adjustments with them. The way in which this adjustment takes place is through actively working with them, through verbal dialogue or concrete substances.

I mentioned earlier that this psychological "making" is mimetic in relation with the psyche's own activity. The psyche is itself a maker, a producer of motions or emotions as well as images. Therapy then is a secondary making, a making with or upon the psyche's primary activity:

> To the extent that I managed to translate the emotions into images—that is to say, to find the images which were concealed in the emotions—I was inwardly calmed and reassured. Had I left those images hidden in the emotions, I might have been torn to pieces by them. There is a chance

---

22. *MDR*, 183.

that I might have succeeded in splitting them off; but in that case I would inexorably have fallen into a neurosis and so been ultimately destroyed by them anyhow. As a result of my experiment I learned how helpful it can be, from the therapeutic point of view, to find the particular images which lie behind emotions.[23]

Unlike Freud, Jung views the psyche's images not as deriving from events or hallucinated wish fulfillments but rather as images in their own right, images of a psychic imagination whose intentions are distinct from the personal ego's wishes or concerns. This notion of the psyche as relatively impersonal is the ground of an imagination as credible as consciousness, and possibly more determinative. When Jung says he "might have been torn to pieces" had he not allowed these images to form, he is attributing a power to the imagination beyond conscious containment. If there is to be stability of any sort, it must be in keeping with the movement and shapings of the psyche itself.

In viewing Jung's making activities as a poiesis mimetic in relation to the psyche's own tendencies, I am not regarding his making as mimetic in relation to any single event of the psyche or its manifestation, since the imagination is more basic than any single manifestation. Nor is Jung's making a copy *of* the psyche, since the psyche and its manifestations are always in motion, always changing.

Jung views the psyche as relational. The archetypes, his basic dominants providing the structural basis of the psyche, appear in accordance with the relationships or "constellations" in given contexts—contexts having to do with the zeitgeist, the ego situation, the environment, other archetypes. Dreams appear in compensatory relationship with consciousness. Symptoms redress

---

23. *MDR*, 177.

a relational imbalance. Figures appear in relational syzygy with other figures.[24] If the psyche is a making activity in motion, psychotherapy must honor that movement with similar activities, activities in keeping with the psyche's "way of operating," relationally and without fixity. What is essential is the process itself. The emphasis is on process rather than product, on the making rather than on what is made.

Herein lies the difference between poiesis as a psychological making and poiesis in the traditional artistic sense, as in the making of a poem.[25] No tangible product results from psychological making, no object for the sake of which the process has been undergone. The focus is rather on the activity of the making--which by no means suggests that evaluation does not enter in, but that the evaluation is appropriate to the unique character of the activity. This issue will be discussed more fully in Chapter Seven.

The idea of the *psyche,* or *anima,* as an ongoing motion (*kinesis*) appears already in Aristotle, who in *De Anima* also relates the psyche with sense-perception (*aisthesis*). This activity of the psyche (*anima*) may even be conceived as independent of physical life, as, for instance, in Homer where psyche is the "breath of life" that escapes from the mouth of a dying hero and continues after death in the form of a ghost.[26] As a vital principle, anima is not literally life, but a movement which appears in life as well as death. This self-motion, as Plato characterizes it (*Phaedrus* 245e),

---

24. For an elaboration of this view of Jung's psychology as relational, see Paul Kugler, *The Alchemy of Discourse* (Lewisburg, Penn.: Bucknell University Press, 1982).

25. James Hillman, "The Pandaemonium of Images: Jung's Contributions to Know Thyself," in his *Healing Fiction* (Thompson, Conn.: Spring Publications, 2019 [1983]), 57–95.

26. Cf. *Iliad* 20.403; *Iliad* 16.148, where "giving up the ghost" (breathing out) is *aistho.*

is the essence (*ousia*) and definition of the soul. For Aristotle even if the soul is not the prime mover, it does remain the final cause of its movement.[27]

Jung uses the term anima in several ways.[28] Anima is a feminine figure in a man's unconscious, and yet she is also a more general function of mediation to the unconscious. She is reflective and elusive, lunar and air-like, moist, attached and close to the earth, the "archetype of life" and yet impersonal and collective as "Anima Mundi"; she is interior as a personal sense of soul and yet external like nature and the elemental world; she is entangling and physical and yet essentially immaterial; she may possess a man's instinctuality and yet without her there is no psyche, imagination, or psychological reflection; she is both life and death, the immediate and the elusive. Establishing relations with her motion and emotions is for Jung a crucial aspect of psychotherapeutic work, for she is the mediation to the unconscious.[29]

We may now view the dove-girl in Jung's dream as a manifestation of this anima. The dove connotes in the Christian tradition spirit and ghost, the Holy Ghost, the "third who walks always beside," *in medias*.[30] The little girl is life and more than life. When her male counterpart is away with the twelve dead she appears in human form, vitally alive. As human and spirit she is of both realms, so that her animation is genuinely of the soul, the psyche as totality.[31] She is imaginally sensate, flinging her arms about

---

27. *De anima* 3.433a-b; *Metaphysics* 1072a-b.

28. Cf. James Hillman, "Anima," *Spring: An Annual of Archetypal Psychology and Jungian Thought* (1973): 97–132; (1974): 113–46, for a compilation of Jung's uses of the notion.

29. Cf. *CW*7: 521, 507; *CW*10: 715; *CW*14: 498n.381.

30. T.S. Eliot, *The Waste Land*, V: 360. For further exposition on the third as ghost, see David L. Miller, "Between God and the Gods—Trinity" in *Eranos Yearbook* 49 (1980): 81–148; cf. also Miller's lecture, "The Holy Ghost and the Grateful Dead," *Eranos Yearbook* 52 (1983): 277–346.

31. *CW*6: 797.

Jung, playing with his children, and yet she is mysteriously, magically "other," a dove descending from and returning to the sky.

Anima as *aisthesis* is also involved in Jung's building activities His making is an animation, and as such a way of knowing and being through an *esse in anima*.[32] The final cause of Jung's activities is the activity itself as well as the vitalization of the child's creative spirit.

All of this points to a most important aesthetic level of Jung's psychology as a making with the soul, poiesis with anima. To view the psyche as a poiesis in anima is to see it as involved in an aesthetic image-making activity. Indeed, according to Jung images are the *sine qua non* of experience.[33] Thus from Jung's psychology one might expect a fully developed discipline of this image-making work.

Such is not the case. In fact this focus on image as an *esse in anima* is only one aspect of Jung's psychology. There are other factors and attitudes at work as well. Jung is also a nineteenth-century scientist, a system builder; he is also a spiritualist concerned with "meanings," wisdom and the beyond. Jung has faces that appear with various effects throughout his career. We shall examine these in a moment.

In addition to the building activities, Jung engaged in imaginal dialogues with psychological figures. Let us look to some primary figures, since Jung's manner of dealing with each of these

---

32. *CW* 6: 66, 77-78, 281. "I am indeed convinced that creative imagination is the only primordial phenomenon accessible to us, the real Ground of the psyche, the only immediate reality. Therefore I speak of *esse in anima*, the only form of being we can experience directly" (Letter to Kurt Plachte, 10 January 1929, in C.G. Jung, *Letters*, vol. 1: *1906-1950*, selected and edited by Gerhard Adler in collaboration with Aniela Jaffé; translated by R.F.C. Hull [Princeton, N.J.: Princeton University Press, 1973], 60).

33. *CW* 6: 750.

shows something of the preferences and conscious predisposi-
tions rooted in his personality.

The first figure that appears to Jung is Elijah, a white bearded,
wise, old man, accompanied by a beautiful young blind woman,
Salome, and a black serpent. According to Jung, Elijah "seemed
to be the most reasonable [vernünftig] of the three, and to have
a clear intelligence." Of Salome Jung was "distinctly suspicious,"
though she and Elijah "had belonged together from all eternity."
Jung characterizes Salome as an erotic anima. figure, "blind
because she does not see the meaning [Sinn] of things." Of the
three, Elijah is the only one with whom Jung engages, because he
considers him "the factor of intelligence and knowledge.[34]

From Elijah another figure develops. Jung calls this figure Philemon and describes him as surrounded by an "Egypto-Hellenis-
tic atmosphere with a Gnostic coloration." Philemon, who "represented superior insight [überlegene Einsicht]," served as teacher
and guru for Jung. Jung and Philemon spent many hours con-
versing over weighty psychological matter.[35]

Later Philemon is "relativized" by the appearance of yet
another figure whom Jung calls "Ka," likening him to the "ka-soul"
of the ancient Egyptian kings, that aspect of the king's embodied
or earthly form. In Jung's fantasy Ka comes "out of the earth as if
out of a deep shaft." In a painting Jung represents him as a herm.
The Ka then is a kind of phallic "spirit of nature."[36] He is also
a craftsman. Jung paints a picture of Ka holding in one hand a
colored pagoda or reliquary, and in the other hand "a stylus with
which he is working on the reliquary."[37] This is the one figure that

---

34. *MDR*, 181.
35. *MDR*, 182.
36. *MDR*, 185.
37. Ibid.

Jung reports having painted, and it is the one figure who is himself a craftsman.[38]

But there is something about Ka that Jung distrusts. Whereas the winged, lame-footed Philemon is concerned with "the spiritual aspect, or 'meaning'" of things, Ka appears somewhat "demonic," more concrete, and aesthetic.

> Ka was he who made everything real, but who also obscured the halcyon spirit, Meaning [den Eisvogelgeist, den Sinn], or replaced it by beauty, the "eternal reflection [ewigen Abglanz]."[39]

With these figures we see something of the tensions in Jung and his preferences. He is distinctly suspicious and will not speak with the erotic anima Salome, for she does not see "meaning." Jung regards Ka, who is connected with beauty, reflection, the physical and concrete, as demonic and obscuring meaning. The only figures Jung actually engages in conversation and affirms without reservation are the wise old men: Elijah, intelligence and knowledge; and Philemon, meaning and spirit.

Though Jung's psyche contains possibilities for an aesthetic elaboration through the concrete sensuousness of the craftsman Ka and the erotic anima elusiveness of Salome, he does not prosecute these possibilities. He prefers instead the more abstract meaning and spirituality of the figures of wisdom. Ka and Salome continue to appear throughout Jung's work, though they never develop fully. Correspondingly, Jung's psychology never developed aesthetically.

The *coup de grace* of this aesthetic possibility is Jung's treatment of a figure he calls "the aesthetic lady [*die ästhetische Dame*]."

---

38. For the significance of the phallic image in Jung's building activities, see Daniel C. Noel, "Veiled Kabir: C. G. Jung's Phallic Self-Image," *Spring: An Annual of Archetypal Psychology and Jungian Thought* (1974): 224–42.

39. *MDR*, 185.

When I was writing down these fantasies, I once asked myself, "What am I really doing? Certainly this has nothing to do with science. But then what is it?" Whereupon a voice within me said, "It is art [*Kunst*]." I was astonished. It had never entered my head that what I was writing had any connection with art. Then I thought, "Perhaps my unconscious is forming a personality that is not me, but which is insisting on coming through to expression." I knew for a certainty that the voice had come from a woman. I recognized it as the voice of a patient, a talented psychopath who had a strong transference to me. She had become a living figure within my mind.[40]

Let us look in some detail at Jung's comment on this figure. In his discussion of Philemon he has explained the nature of unconscious personalities, noting them as autonomous and imaginally distinct from the ego. There is a peculiar naivete in his musing once again, "perhaps my unconscious is forming a personality that is not me," as though he had never before observed this phenomenon.

Also notable is the immediate association of this voice with the voice of a patient. In his earlier imaginations Jung had valued the voices as realities in them selves. Associations, if they appeared, came later. But here Jung immediately labels the voice as belonging to a person he already knows and has diagnosed as a psychopath.[41] Jung continues:

---

40. Ibid.

41. Jung never reveals the identity of this patient whom he calls "the aesthetic woman." But there are similarities in his descriptions of her that match what we know of Sabina Spielrein, a patient he treated at Burghölzli and with whom he was later intimately involved. See Aldo Carotenuto, *A Secret Symmetry: Sabina Spielrein between Jung and Freud,* translated by Arno Pomerans, John Shepley, and Krishna Winston (New York: Pantheon Books, 1982). Both the aesthetic woman and Spielrein were patients with whom Jung also had a more personal relationship. He credits both as having in-

Obviously what I was doing wasn't science [*Wissenschaft*].
What then could it be but art? It was as though these were
the only alternatives in the world. That is the way a woman's
mind works.[42]

Jung generally attributes a dichotomous either-or mentality to
inferior thinking, sometimes to logical thinking in general, but
here he chauvinistically attributes this primitive mode to the
feminine mind.

I said very emphatically to this voice that my fantasies had
nothing to do with art, and I felt a great inner resistance. No
voice came through, however, and I kept on writing. Then
came the next assault, and again the same assertion: "That is
art." This time I caught her and said, "No, it is not art! On the
contrary, it is nature," and prepared myself for an argument.
When nothing of the sort occurred, I reflected that "the
woman within me [*die Frau in mir*]" did not have the speech
centres I had. And so I suggested that she use mine. She did
so and came through with a long statement.[43]

Jung never reports to us what this statement is, perhaps sparing
us more of his own recasting. (She is using *his* "speech centers.")
And perhaps this aesthetic female figure is not given to verbal
dialectic, preferring other modes of expression.[44]

---

troduced him to the notion of the "anima." In addition both were clearly
aesthetic types. In her diary, Spielrein euphemistically refers to her intima-
cies with Jung as their "poetry"! See also Bruno Bettelheim, "Scandal in the
Family," *New York Review of Books* (30 June 1983): 9–44. Bettelheim criti-
cizes Jung's callous treatment of Spielrein and points out his denials and
devaluations of the relationship.

42. *MDR*, 185.

43. *MDR*, 185–86.

44. Cf. Jung's *Psychology of the Unconscious*, translated by Beatrice M.
Hinkle (London: Kegan Paul, 1919), 7ff., where Jung ties speech to directed
thinking, of which science is the highest achievement, and relegates fantasy thinking to a non-linguistic mode, which "turns away from reality, sets
free subjective wishes, and is, in regard to adaptation, wholly unproductive."

Jung's insistence that he is involved not with art but with nature leads us to wonder what he means by nature [*Natur*].[45] Most probably, in keeping with a Western convention, he is regarding nature as a stable object, a given which may then be explored. From an aesthetic point of view, this assumption of nature as a fixed objectification need not, as Richard Rorty contends, imply epistemological or metaphysical guarantees, but may be simply the constancy by which a better story is told.[46]

Another habit of the conceptual Jung is to speak of events as though they contained contrary poles, negative and positive. These oppositions divide and isolate events in terms of simplistic negative-positive valuations. In a more aesthetic attitude Jung might speak of an event's ambiguity or complexity, noting its contrasts and tensions. We will look later at Jung's use of oppositional thinking and its effects.

It is also notable that Jung's aesthetic anima figure has no visible image form but seems to him an "invisible presence." Perhaps invisible because she has not been "seen" by Jung, the anima becomes a vague, amorphous presence. Elsewhere Jung notes the aesthetic as important precisely for its ability to give shape, form, and clarity.[47]

Nonetheless, fantasy thinking is related to aesthetic thinking and is the means by which the ancient, mythical mind operated (cf. pp. 12–13) .

45. For a listing of significant normative meanings for the term nature, see Arthur O. Lovejoy and George Boas, "Appendix: Some Meanings of 'Nature,'" in their *Primitivism and Related Ideas in Antiquity* (New York: Octagon, 1965), 447–56.

46. Richard Rorty, *Philosophy and the Mirror of Nature* (Princeton, N.J.: Princeton University Press, 1979), 344–45, and as discussed in Jonathan Culler, *On Deconstruction: Theory and Criticism after Structuralism* (Ithaca, New York: Cornell University Press, 1982), 77ff.

47. Cf. *CW* 8: 179, where Jung notes the importance of the aesthetic in giving form; *CW* 8: 167 where he speaks of it as clarifying affect. Jung views

> Then a new idea came to me: in putting down all this mate-
> rial for analysis I was in effect writing letters to the anima,
> that is, to a part of myself wit a different viewpoint from my
> conscious one. I got remarks of an unusual and unexpected
> character. I was like a patient in analysis with a ghost and a
> woman [bei einem weiblichen Geist]![48]

Jung now speaks of the anima as though she were the unconscious in general, which indeed accords with one of his later
descriptions of her as the "life behind consciousness...from
which...consciousness arises."[49] The effect here, however, is that
the actual figure of the anima gets replaced with a general notion
about her. The result is ghostly—a strange irony since, as noted in
the dove-girl dream, the anima *is* part ghost. Her ghostly aspect
attests to a more than human quality; the anima is beyond life
(and thus not identical with the woman Jung knows). In fact, here
Jung is a patient of the anima. "I was like a patient in analysis..."
But Jung does not submit as a patient; his conscious viewpoint
does not alter. Rather than learn from the figure he moves off
into theoretical speculation. Here Jung uses this notion of nature
as an either-or to effectively block the aesthetic anima. Either it
is nature *or* it is art, with no possibility of a place between. Jung
continues:

> I was greatly intrigued by the fact that a woman should inter-
> fere with me from within. My conclusion was that she must
> be the "soul," in the primitive sense, and I began to speculate
> on the reasons why the name "anima" was given to the soul.
> Why was it thought of as feminine? Later I came to see that
> this inner feminine figure plays a typical, or archetypal, role
> in the unconscious of a man, and I called her the "anima."

---

form and understanding as opposed (*CW*8: 176ff) and the psychic process
as proceeding through an alternation between the two (*CW*8: 179).

   48. *MDR*, 186.

   49. *CW*9.1: 57.

The corresponding figure in the unconscious of woman I called the "animus."[50]

Rather than listen to or explore the "soul" Jung speculates about it—"why the name 'anima'?" "Why was it thought of as feminine?" It must be archetypal. This move from abstract musing on the event to a typing of it is characteristic of Jung in his scientific mode. Not infrequently he goes on to construct a corresponding concept, here the "animus" in women, to balance the situation he has set up. The balance becomes objectified as anima-animus, male and female, and Jung the observer is removed from the situation.[51]

It is not unusual for a person involved in active imagination (particularly for one not yet skilled in it as Jung, since he was inventing it, was not) to go off into conceptual thought, forgetting the figure. But this report, we must remember is a recollection. Jung has had some forty years to reflect on and reassess the situation, yet this particular complex remains unmoved.

At first it was the negative aspect of the anima that most impressed me. I felt a little awed by her. It was like the feeling of an invisible presence in the room.[52]

Speculation leads to generalization. "I got remarks of an unusual and unexpected character." Jung never says what these unusual, unexpected remarks were. He gives us no significant details. The anima has become for him no longer a precise presence, but now ghostly in another sense—insubstantial, disembodied, haunting.

---

50. *MDR*, 186.

51. See "The Dogma of Gender," in my *Echo's Subtle Body: Contributions to an Archetypal Psychology* (Thompson, Conn.: Spring Publications, 2017 [1982]), 39-52, for a discussion of the implications of this kind of thinking.

52. *MDR*, 186.

In the following passage Jung tells how he wrote out his fantasies in order to instruct the anima and to keep her from twisting them into intrigues.

> Every evening I worked on my notes, for I thought if I did not write to the anima, she would not be able to grasp my fantasies...By writing them out, the anima could not spin them into intrigues [*sie konnte keine Intrigen daraus spinnen*].[53]

We noted earlier how for Jung the actual forming and shaping of psychic contents is essential to psychotherapeutic work. Here he implies that this activity gives him a grounding separate from the anima. ("Es gab aber noch einen anderen Grund für meine Gewissenhaftigkeit.") From this other ground (*anderen Grund*) and conscientiousness (*Gewissenhaftigkeit*), Jung gives the anima a way of under standing or grasping (*fassen*) his fantasies, rather than spinning them into intrigues. In a sense, therefore, Jung's activities instruct and "upgrade" the anima, so that she becomes less primitive and simply destructive. The activity of making now becomes an ethical discipline necessary to psychological development, which leads more resolutely to an emphasis on consciousness.[54]

> Often, as I was writing, I would have peculiar reactions that threw me off. Only slowly did I learn to distinguish between myself [*meinen Gedanken*] and the interruption [*den Inhalten der Stimme*]. When something emotionally *vulgar or banal* came up, I would say to myself, "It is perfectly true that I have thought and felt this way at some time or other, but I don't have to think and feel that way now. I need not accept this banality of mine in perpetuity; that is an unnecessary humiliation [*wozu diese Demütigung*]?"

---

53. Ibid.; translation modified.
54. Jung speaks of psychological work as "upgrading" the psyche's libido. Cf. "On Psychic Energy," in *CW* 8: 3–66.

The essential thing is to differentiate oneself from these unconscious contents by personifying them, and at the same time to bring them into relationship with consciousness. That is the technique for stripping them of their power. It is not too difficult to personify them, as they always possess a certain degree of autonomy, a separate identity of their own. Their autonomy is a most uncomfortable thing to reconcile oneself to, and yet the very fact that the unconscious presents itself in that way gives us the best means of handling it [*Und doch liegt gerade hierin die Möglichkeit, mit dem Unbewußten umzugehen*].[55]

In distinguishing between his thoughts (*Gedanken*) and the voice of the anima (*Inhalten der Stimme*) and then judging her banalities on the basis of this, Jung is evaluating her from a position with which he is identified ("my thoughts"), i.e., an unreflected ego stance.

There is a difference between working on the anima from a self-identified (ego) position and from the position of a craftsman. As a craftsman one is within a metaphorical or aesthetic reality; as ego-identified one is the reality. The difficulty with Jung's identification is that it denies the "other" her more organic possibilities of form and differentiation. After all it is the anima, not his thoughts, who portends Jung's aesthetic sensibility.

By assuming the task of valuing and forming to be guided by the intellect with which he identifies, Jung blocks the possibility of unknown, more subtle aesthetic patterns. Evaluation and judgment remain with the thinking ego. This ego, whose province the aesthetic is not (rather than the anima whose province it is) decides what is "banal" and "vulgar." And these judgments, Jung admits, are made defensively, to strip the *anima* of her "power" and to avoid "unnecessary humiliation."

---

55. *MDR*, 186–87; translation modified.

Jung's defensiveness prevents any conscious influence of the anima. His sympathies are with Philemon and Elijah, prizing values of spiritual meaning and system (mandalas, Eastern metaphysics), to which he tends to place the aesthetic in opposition. Consequently his stance is generally non-aesthetic or even anti-aesthetic.

In Jung's aesthetic criticism, particularly in his paper on Joyce's *Ulysses,* his interest is drawn to symbolizations and themes, which he then parallels with more ancient material.[56] In "Psychology and Literature" he distinguishes sharply between personal "psychological art" and the more profound "visionary art," clearly preferring the latter.[57] He speaks of story as "only a means...for capturing a meaningful content.[58] In these articles Jung excuses himself from artistic evaluation, maintaining the job of the psychologist is to explain "meanings" that touch the primordial depths of art—which depths are "word less and imageless," basically abstract.[59] In Jung's notion of art and interpretation there is no place for phenomenal, "ordinary," concrete immediacies. Art must be "visionary" with "meaningful contents" or it is of little interest. He disregards technical proficiency and matters of form, and goes so far as to state that bad art may be most psychologically interesting.[60] "Indeed, literary products of highly dubious merit are often of the greatest interest to the psychologist."[61] By drawing the aesthetic and the meaningful apart, Jung implies that the psychologist should not be concerned with the aesthetic.

---

56. "'Ulysses': A Monologue," in *CW* 15, pp. 109–34.

57. "Psychology and Literature [*Psychologie und Dichtung*], in *CW* 15, pp. 84–105.

58. *CW* 15: 143.

59. *CW* 15: 151.

60. See Graham Hough, "Poetry and the Anima," *Spring: An Annual of Archetypal Psychology and Jungian Thought* (1973): 85–96.

61. *CW* 15: 136.

As we mentioned earlier, the aesthetic anima was not only an internal psychic figure for Jung. She was also an actual woman, a patient with whom he was involved. He saw this relationship as an interference to his own development, and reports having broken with her in order to emerge from his depression.[62]

Later while serving in the military, Jung received a letter from "that aesthetic lady." At the time he was engaged in a self-therapy which involved the drawing of mandalas.

> I sketched every morning in a notebook a small circular drawing, a mandala, which seemed to correspond to my inner situation at the time. With the help of these drawings I could observe my psychic transformations from day to day. One day...I received a letter from that aesthetic lady [*jener ästhetischen Dame*], in which she again stubbornly maintained that the fantasies arising from my unconscious had artistic value and should be considered art. The letter got on my nerves. It was far from stupid and therefore dangerously persuasive. The modern artist, after all, seeks to create art out of the unconscious. The utilitarianism and self importance concealed behind this thesis touched a doubt in myself, namely, my uncertainty as to whether the fantasies I was producing were really spontaneous and natural, and not ultimately my own arbitrary inventions. I was by no means free from the bigotry and hubris of consciousness which wants to believe that any half-way decent inspiration is due to one's own merit, whereas inferior reactions come merely by chance, or even derive from alien sources. Out of this irritation and disharmony within myself there proceeded, the following day, a changed mandala: part of the periphery had burst open and the symmetry was destroyed.[63]

Jung's aesthetic anima is destructive of his systematic, mandala-making quality of mind. She upsets his symmetries and ruptures

---

62. *MDR*, 194.
63. *MDR*, 195.

his symbolic self-containment. That this destruction of system may be one of the legitimate functions of art, and of the creative psyche, does not here occur to Jung. Though at other times he will speak of the value of such interruptions, at this time he was in no state of mind to appreciate it.[64] His concern at the moment was to pull himself together, and the geometric regularity of mandala structures served this self-containing function.

Jung goes on in this passage to describe the mandala as symbolizing "Formation, Transformation, Eternal Mind's eternal recreation," which he characterizes as the wholeness of the "self—that is, my whole being—actively at work."[65] But is it? Is not the anima part of this "whole being"? Is she not at work—in this case, in breaking his mandalas? Jung seems to have identified himself with an idea represented geometrically by the mandala. By orient ing from what he considers the goal of psychic life, he embraces an abstraction before the fact. This abstraction results in a closure, as though life and its goals were already formed and outside the stream of life, no longer subject to life's discontinuities, emotions, and entanglements. The mandala is static and geometric. It represents a spiritual goal about life rather than life in the living; it is an abstraction and generalization rather than life as concrete particularities and unexpected ambiguities.[66] In turning to symbolic idea in lieu of actual phenomena, Jung rejects the aesthetic anima as destructive—and of course she is, to the systematic mode he seeks to maintain. Thus the wisdom of

----

64. Cf. *CW* 15: 172, 175, 180–90.

65. *MDR*, 196.

66. Cf. James Hillman on the mandala as a defense, in "Dionysus in Jung's Writings," *Spring: An Annual of Archetypal Psychology and Jungian Thought* (1972): 198–99; see also Robert Creeley's distinction between metaphysical and phenomenological perception, as recorded by William V. Spanos, "Talking with Robert Creeley," *Boundary 2,* vol. 6/7 (Spring-Autumn 1978): 61.

Philemon translates in Jung as an attitude that values wholeness and abstract meaning before the actual event.

Meaning serves Jung defensively. By wisely knowing and understanding the meaning of figures before their actual appearance he can dispense with the figures them selves. Such is the case with the aesthetic anima:

> Today I no longer need these conversations with the anima, for I no longer have such emotions...Today I am directly conscious of the anima's ideas because I have learned to accept the contents of the unconscious and to understand them. I know how I must behave towards the inner images. I can read their meaning directly from my dreams, and therefore no longer need a mediator [*Vermittlerin*] to communicate them.[67]

According to Jung's statement here, he no longer needs anima figures because he is "directly conscious" of and already understands any ideas the anima may have. The hubris of this attitude appears in a later passage as Jung's projections concerning the nature of art. The modern artist, according to Jung, attempts "to create art out of the unconscious." This attempt is utilitarian [*Utilitarismus*] and self-important [*Wichtigtuerei*]. Such art consists of "arbitrary inventions" [*arbiträre Leistung*], inviting "bigotry" [*Vorurteil*] and a "hubris of consciousness" [*Hybris des Bewußtseins*].[68]

These statements concerning art are so extreme and in such contradiction to Jung's attitudes expressed elsewhere that we must regard them as peculiar to the present context and constellation.[69] Jung's identification with mandala consciousness

67. *MDR*, 188.
68. Ibid., 195.
69. Cf. "Is there a Freudian Type of Poetry?," in *CW*18, pp. 765–66; "On the Relation of Analytical Psychology to Poetry," in *CW*15, pp. 65–83; "Psychology and Literature," in ibid., pp. 84–105.

claims a superiority that has blinded his ability to self-reflect. The hubris of his position appears in his unconsciousness of art. What he projects as the dangers of art—its arbitrariness, utility, self-importance, bigotry, hubris—are far more apt descriptions of his own position. After all it is he who denies the aesthetic anima, he who claims power over her. Her only crime has been to say "it is art."

Jung's objections to art are also ethical:

> What the anima said seemed to me full of a deep cunning. If I had taken these fantasies of the unconscious as art, they would have carried no more conviction than visual percep- tions, as if I were watching a movie. I would have felt no moral obligation toward them. The anima might then have easily seduced me into believing that I was a misunderstood artist, and that my so-called artistic nature gave me the right to neglect reality. If I had followed her voice, she would in all probability have said to me one day, "Do you imagine the nonsense you're engaged in is really art? Not a bit." Thus the insinuations of the anima, the mouthpiece of the uncon- scious [*Sprachrohr des Unbewußten*], can utterly destroy a man. In the final analysis the decisive factor is always con- sciousness, which can understand the manifestations of the unconscious and take up a position towards them.[70]

Jung regards this aspect of the anima her "negative side." As such she creates seductive, illusionary inflations. Had he listened to her, he would have come to believe himself a "misunderstood artist." Certainly this inflation would have been dangerous—but no more so than any other inflation. Had he believed himself a misunderstood visionary or prophet, his belief would have been equally ungrounded.

Elsewhere, Jung stresses the importance of reliable conscious- ness for persons in professional roles, contrasting this situation

---

70. *MDR*, 187.

with that of artists and creative persons in whom the partition between conscious and unconscious is irresponsibly permeable.[71] Since artists are presumably less reliable, Jung feels justified in guarding himself from artistic illusions. As a physician responsible for others he must abjure the self-indulgences that accompany artistic dispositions.

Armed with this preconception concerning the irresponsibility of artistry, Jung judges the aesthetic anima as "negative" and dangerous. Were he to allow the aesthetic, he would become "only aesthetic," lost in "an all-enveloping phantasmagoria" without a moral sense of responsibility.[72] From the position with which Jung has identified, he claims all morality as his own such that there is no possibility for an *Auseinandersetzung* with the anima. He has already decided what morality consists in, and where it is located. Hence he knows before even engaging the anima that she is negative, dangerous, and that if he listens to her he will become merely passive, without "conviction" or "moral obligation."

This attitude of moral preemptiveness contrasts with Jung's attitude elsewhere, as when he notes that "unconscious contents want first of all to be seen clearly, which can only be done by giving them shape, and to be judged only when everything they have to say is tangibly present.[73] Or again, "the less the initial material is shaped and developed, the greater is the danger that understanding will be governed not by the empirical facts but by theoretical and moral considerations.[74]

The tension between the aesthetic and the ethical is not to be easily resolved. In *Creative Intuition in Art and Poetry* Maritain distinguishes between the morality of doing (*agibilia*) and the art

---

71. *CW* 8: 135.
72. *CW* 8, p. 68
73. *CW* 8: 179.
74. *CW* 8: 180.

of making (*factibilia*). Though not a moral virtue, art is nonetheless a virtue because,

> in the larger and more philosophical sense the ancients
> gave this word: a habitus or "state of possession," an inner
> strength developed in man, which perfects him with regard
> to his ways of acting, and makes him—to the extent to
> which he uses it—undeviating in a given activity...Art is
> a virtue of the practical intellect—that particular virtue
> of the practical intellect which deals with the creation of
> objects to be made.[75]

Following Maritain, Jung might well have risked the aesthetic
without losing his soul. Indeed, he would have been engaged in
a virtuous activity. His morality or "moral obligation" would have
been an issue to be dealt with separately, but artistic engagement
would not have obviated this possibility.

Jung maintains that had he allowed the anima's suggestion,
his fantasies would have been no more than "visual perceptions."
This distrust of the visually sensate assumes that such could exist
devoid of all other qualities or meanings, as if the sensate were
of a different order from meaning and intelligibility. We can find
this attitude denigrating the sensate in Jung's description of the
"sensation type," that individual who may be so caught in the concrete that "the events in his life hardly deserve the name 'experience' at all."[76]

Jung's concern that his fantasies would have been only "visual
perceptions," that is, sensate events without "experience" is indeed
ironic since the anima herself was invisible. How could it be that
the very problem with this invisible figure is that she produces
only in the realm of visible perceptions? The conundrum Jung
inadvertently expresses points to a complex at the root of the

---

75. Maritain, *Creative Intuition in Art and Poetry*, 49.
76. *CW*6: 606.

aesthetic anima. She *is* both invisible and visible. The complex is a concatenation of both.

To read the complex from within, we might say that the invisible hides a potential visibility as well, and conversely the perceptually visible contains an invisibility. In art this invisibility, this "something more" within perception, has been called by various names. Valéry calls this invisibility the "aesthetic infinite"; Maritain terms it "the inner being of things, or poetry"; Plato calls it *mousikē*.[77]

This "something more" within the perceptual also fits Jung's descriptions of the anima or soul in general, as we saw earlier. But when Jung is suspicious of the anima, as he is here, perception too becomes suspect—a mere passivity without conviction, an interiority without soul.

Jung's disavowal of an aesthetic figure leads him back to the tradition of rational prejudices regarding sensation and perception—which prejudices contradict other attitudes we find in Jung. More characteristic of Jung is his emphasis on "psychic body," the feminine, the dark fourth, which he considers missing in the Christian trinity. This fourth is also emphasized in his insistence on the substantial "shadow" of psychic attitude; and functions, in his emphasis on "instinct" as the basis of archetypes, as well as in his volumes devoted to the physical substances and trans formations of alchemy.[78]

Clearly these are distinct attitudes and sympathies in Jung. One embraces the aesthetic, affirms the senses and the sensuous imagination. When in this mode, Jung is *homo faber*—a maker in sympathy with the psyche's own processes. Grounded in a realm

---

77. Maritain, *Creative Intuition in Art and Poetry*, 3.

78. See "instinct," in *CW* 8: 277, and the essays on alchemy in *CW* 9.2, *CW* 12, *CW* 13, and *CW* 14.

that is both sensuous and imaginal, an interim realm of *esse in anima,* Jung is drawn to the concrete and particular as at once visible and invisible.

This Jung is a phenomenologist, in that he deals with whatever appears as it appears; he is aesthetic in that he affirms the sensate and the perceptual; he is poetic in that he engages as a maker with the psyche.

But there is a second Jung, a Jung drawn to system and meaning. In this attitude, Jung considers the sensate merely passive, the aesthetic without obligation, the anima seductive and inflating. This Jung views the feminine as a spinner of intrigues, and adopts a willful stance toward her. His intention is to manage and educate this figure, denying her persuasive power over him. In countering her, however, he also loses her phenomenal significance as a psychic figure. She no longer has value in herself, she is no longer a content, an other to whom he must listen and respond.

Identifying with the mandala representation of whole ness, Jung substitutes a geometric abstraction for the particularity of actual phenomena—the anima's actual appearance. Meaning comes before occurrence, abstraction before event. The resulting totalization of psychic experience obviates the particular, the anima, and the aesthetic. The unexpected is viewed as a threat, a destructive force, rather than as a harbinger of psychic value and potential.

Psychologically, the denied does not cease to exist- particularly a content as powerful, vital, and seductive as the aesthetic anima is for Jung. She continues to have effect throughout his work—though this effect is often contrary to Jung's intention and obscured by his conscious positions. As an unconscious factor the anima contaminates Jung's attempts to be systematically contained and expositorily clear. The result in Jung's work is a mixture of sudden insight and systematic intent, neither a fully developed poetic nor a wholly successful system. His work is contradictory and difficult to follow, because there are two forces at work—one insisting on meaning, the other on making.

The following chapter addresses Jung's earliest published; work, his medical dissertation. Jung's effort in this paper is to be as systematic and scientific as befits a research treatise. He documents his evidence and notes the relevant literature. If we look more carefully into the situation, however, we note some peculiarities and obvious lapses in his scientific method and stated intentions.

CHAPTER TWO

"On the Psychology and Pathology
of So-Called Occult Phenomena":
A Case Report as Fiction

Jung was again and again drawn to the study of unusual topics. The odd event that did not fit usual classifications or ways of thinking was for him frequently most interesting. His medical thesis, which one might expect to have been his most scientific and academic undertaking, took on the study of occult phenomena, a topic avoided at the time by positivist science as not deserving serious attention.

In "On the Psychology and Pathology of So-Called Occult Phenomena," written while he was an assistant to Eugen Bleuler at Burghölzli, Jung relates a series of encounters with a fifteen-year-old mediumistic girl, whom he calls "S.W."[1] The seance sessions, which Jung personally attended, involved episodes of somnambulism, automatic writing, periodic amnesia, communication with spirits, table moving, speaking in tongues, trance states, cryptomnesia, and other such spiritualist phenomena, at the time not solidly classified as medical syndromes.

Jung's stated intention was to study these phenomena objectively in order to place them within a scientific frame. Hence throughout the dissertation he compares and contrasts the various paranormal states with known pathological phenomena of hysterical distractibility, abnormal dream states, various forms of amnesia, and so on.

---

1. "Zur Psychologie und Pathologie sogenannter occulter Phänomene" (1902), in *CW* 1, pp. 3–88.

On the other hand, it was also evidently Jung's desire that the case of S.W. not settle ultimately into pathological categories.[2]

> ...certain features point beyond pathological inferiority to something more than a merely analogical relationship with the phenomena of normal psychology, and even with the psychology of the supernormal [*Psychologie des Mehrwertigen*], that of genius.[3]

Not only does Jung refuse a strict reduction to pathology, he even emphasizes differences from normal states, insisting that his case shows "something more than a merely analogical relationship with the phenomena of normal psychology." In fact, S.W.'s psychology suggested to Jung another basis entirely, a basis he characterizes as "super normal," and more like the psychology of genius.

By inflating the implications of his case, Jung separates it from usual classifications and modes of consideration. The interpretive attitude implied is one which uses the extraordinary, the uncommon, to understand the usual, the unknown to understand the known, rather than the more classic tendency to understand the unknown in terms of the known. The case he is to describe "is not very common, and it is worth while to examine such cases more closely, as they sometimes afford us a wealth of interesting observations."[4]

This elevation of the unusual is typical of depth psychology at the turn of the century. Its pioneers—Flournoy, Myers, Binet, Delboeuf, Janet, Charcot, Bernheim, James, Breuer, Freud—were all drawn to the study of unusual events: spiritualism, somnambulism, mediumship, automatic writing, cryptomnesia, and other bizarre behaviors.

---

2. *CW*1: 3–5.
3. *CW*1: 3.
4. *CW*1: 5.

The most notable for the future of depth psychology were those that came to be called "hysterical," and which provided the case material for the early studies of Charcot, Breuer, and Freud. Hysterical enactments were important for depth psychology in that they helped to challenge early psychiatry's materialistic and positivist underpinnings.

By studying odd behaviors with doubtful or undemonstrable physiological basis, depth psychology was able to formulate for itself a position apart from physiological materialism. The physical body became a body driven by wishes and desires, the human being a creature of fantasies and disguised enactments.

Psychopathology, once considered physiologically caused, became the psychopathology of neuroses, explainable by psychological mechanisms of defense. The psyche, according to Freud, desired fulfillment of its wishes but denied that fulfillment through its defenses.

Freud tended to view these wishes and their defenses rather literally, as though they were the actual "facts" of the psyche (and hence his view the only one possible). Jung regarded Freud as replacing the medical materialism he opposed with his own brand of literalism.

From Jung's point of view certain neurotic behaviors might best be seen in terms of these underlying defense mechanisms, but other visions were also possible. Jung's position was more relative in regard to psychopathology, as we see in the following passage from his 1917 essay "On the Psychology of the Unconscious."

> For my part, I had the great advantage over both Freud and
> Adler of not having grown up within the narrow confines of
> a psychology of the neuroses; rather, I approach them from
> the side of psychiatry, prepared for modern psychology by
> Nietzsche, and apart from Freud's views I also had before
> my eyes the growth of the views of Adler. In this way I found
> myself in the thick of the conflict from the very beginning,

and was forced to regard not only the existing opinions, but my own as well, as relative...[5]

By grounding his psychology not in the neuroses (explicable by the mechanisms of substitution and displacement), but in the more essential psychoses, Jung felt he was dealing with deeper phenomena, revealed in the breakdown of structures of being and belief, hence his reference to Nietzschean relativity.

Jung credits his doctoral case as evidencing this deeper and more independent level of psychic reality, and for this reason, characterizes the study as essential to the formation of his own view:

> Just as the Breuer case...was decisive for Freud, so a decisive experience underlies my own views. Towards the end of my medical training I observed for a long period a case of somnambulism in a young girl. It became the theme of my doctor's dissertation. For one acquainted with my scientific writings it may not be without interest to compare this forty-year-old study with my later ideas.[6]

In his 1935 preface to "The Relations Between the Ego and the Unconscious," Jung again attributes his view of the unconscious psyche as having resulted from his observations of S.W.:

> This idea of the independence of the unconscious, which distinguishes my views so radically from those of Freud, came to me as far back as 1902, when I was engaged in studying the psychic history of a young girl somnambulist.[7]

In viewing the unconscious as "independent" Jung meant to establish a perspective on psychic processes such that interpretation of them could not revert, as with Freud's interpretations, to established mechanistic laws—whether psychological or physiological. If the unconscious is independent of what

---

5. *CW7*: 199
6. Ibid.
7. Ibid., p. 123.

is already known, interpretation must move beyond the confines of established laws toward unknown and, for Jung, less material meanings.

Whereas Freud observed in his cases a libidinous, sexual basis for the psyche, Jung's observations did not lead him to the same conclusions. Psychic libido was for him not primarily sexual but pointed toward other realms as well. In the case of S.W. this realm was well beyond the physical body, sometimes to its detriment. When S.W. entered her mediumistic states, her body paled. According to Jung, "an almost constant feature was the sudden pallor which gave her face a waxen anaemic hue that was positively frightening."[8]

As the life blood was drained from his subject's body, she seemed to Jung to be "wafted to distant places where the spirits led her."[9] These "spirits" appeared to be nonmaterial and life-threatening. S.W. felt "she would probably die in one of these attacks, that her soul only hung on to her body by a very thin thread, so that her body could scarcely go on living."[10]

This loss of physical body, its anaemic paling, presaged the entrance of another kind of body in the guise of psychological "spirits," "other personalities," who conversed and performed with animation. As the physical body receded, the psychological body, composed of various personalities, seemed to take on life.

Jung characterizes this transition from the physical to the psychological as a turning point. He uses words like "sudden" or "suddenly" [plötzlich] to describe the transition from one realm to the other. A "sudden pallor" would show on S.W.'s face.[11] As the figures began to form, "the room would suddenly light up."[12]

---

8. *CW*1: 40.
9. *CW*1: 42.
10. *CW*1: 40.
11. Ibid.
12. *CW*1: 43.

"Suddenly" S.W. would begin speaking "in an altered, deep tone of voice."[13] "Suddenly" her grammar would shift to the third person.[14]

Jung mirrors imagistically the tension between S.W. and her figures through contrasts of dark and light.

> Darkness came on...Suddenly S.W. became very agitated, jumped up nervously, fell on her knees, and cried: "There, there, don't you see that *light,* that *star* there?" She grew more all the more excited, and called for a *lamp* in terror.[15]

The figures appeared "shining white" in "white veil-like robes." The states were characterized by "hypnagogic brightness [*Helligkeit*] and "seeing sparks" whereas S.W. herself "always preferred the darkness."[16]

Jung describes the observed events with a vividness and drama in contrast to his stance as analytic reporter, which is at a dispassionate remove. Throughout his case report Jung's attitude is that of an objective observer, as though he were merely reporting, comparing, and attempting systematically to place the behavior he is witnessing.

But as noted earlier, something in Jung does not wish to categorize these events irrevocably. So in the manner of his exposition we find a peculiar undoing, as if Jung both attempts yet resists his delineations of the phenomena. From the beginning he has difficulty getting into the topic. He spends fourteen pages of introduction detailing instances with no more than tangential relevance to his case. He goes on to divide his material into four main sections with numerous subsections, but these are largely interchangeable and constantly overlap, repeating material he has already mentioned. The result is a thwarted circularity,

---

13. *CW*1: 48.
14. Ibid.
15. *CW*1: 45.
16. *CW*1: 43.

belying the intent of his organization. Superimposition rests upon superimposition, obscuring the linear, logical exposition.

As in the previous chapter, it is as if there are two Jungs operative, each unaware of the other. One is objective, systematic and intentional, a scientist; the other is engaged with a welter of autonomous, vital and confusing "personalities." This second Jung is subjectively involved and, one suspects, fascinated with his case.

Jung was not unaware of the role of personal involvement and subjectivity in scientific writing in general. Indeed, in his autobiography he admits that recognition of this subjective factor is what turned him to the study of psychiatry.

> My violent reaction set in when Krafft-Ebing spoke of the "subjective character" of psychiatric textbooks. So, I thought, the textbook is in part the subjective confession of the author. With his specific prejudice, with the totality of his being, he stands behind the objectivity of his experiences and responds to the "disease of the personality" with the whole of his own personality.[17]

Jung's "specific prejudice" in the case of S.W. had to do with his personal and familial involvement in the case. S.W. was a pseudonym for Helena (Helly) Preiswerk, who was Jung's first cousin. Her father and his mother were brother and sister, so he and Helly shared the same grand parents, Samuel and Auguste Preiswerk-Faber.

According to the recent disclosures of another relative, Stephanie Zumstein-Preiswerk, it was Jung who organized these seances, which were held in his mother's living room around the mysteriously cracked oak table of the grandfather.[18] These grandparents were spiritualist-minded, eccentric people.

---

17. *MDR*, 109.

18. In his autobiography Jung attributes the sudden splitting of this table (along with the snapping of the blade of a bread knife) as priming his interest for seances (*MDR*, 105–6).

In his report Jung describes his case as that of "a a girl with poor inheritance"—ironic when one realizes this "poor inheritance" is also Jung's. In detailing the family's peculiarities he characterizes the grandmother as a "peculiar, odd character," who after a feverish illness in her youth went into a trance from which she did not awaken "until the crown of her head was burnt with a red-hot iron." Thereafter throughout her life she had fainting fits and somnambulistic episodes in which she uttered prophecies.

The grandfather, who also served as the major "control" figure in the sessions with S.W., was similarly fey. He was head of the reformed clergy in Basel. Every week at a fixed hour he held "conversations" with his deceased first wife. Jung's mother as a child had the task of standing behind her father in order to protect him from spirits who attempted to disturb him as he was writing his sermons.[19]

Besides the grandparental inheritance, Jung specifies the grandfather's brother, who is feeble-minded, eccentric and sees visions, the grandfather's sister (likewise "peculiar" and "odd"), and S.W.'s father (Jung's uncle), and two brothers who have "waking hallucinations." What Jung describes as significant for his subject's pathology is not irrelevant for his own.

Jung's maternal line was of great importance for him emotionally and psychologically. In his autobiography he states that it was through his mother that he first learned of secondary, "autonomous" personalities (what he calls her "personality No. 2").[20] He also credits his mother with a natural sense, archaic and uncanny, from which he inherited the gift of perceiving by way of an instinctual "participation mystique," entailing a dissolution of personal

---

19. Aniela Jaffé, *Jung's Last Years and Other Essays*, translated by R.F.C. Hull and Murray Stein (Dallas: Spring Publications, 1984 [1971], 2.

20. MDR, 45.

boundaries and conscious limitations so that awareness spreads impersonally, in participation with one's surroundings. According to Jung, in this state it is "as if the 'eyes of the background' do the seeing."[21] In his case study, S.W. and her autonomous personalities become these "eyes of the background," the dissociated awareness from which Jung in his objective, scientific disguise is apparently removed.

Interesting contradictions and duplicities come to light, however, when one compares Jung's account of the situation surrounding the seances with the accounts given by others. As noted above there is evidence to suggest that Jung himself organized the sittings—a suspicion that contrasts with his pretense of having attended them as outside observer.[22] As the older cousin, Jung seems to have played a key role in initiating Helly into her mediumistic activities. He had read "virtually the whole of the literature available" on spiritualism-and had inscribed a copy of Justinus Kerner's *Seherin von Prevorst* to Helene on her fifteenth birthday. just before he began his "study" of her.[23] Rather than a carefully circumscribed empirical study lasting two years, as Jung claims, according to Zumstein-Preiswerk the sessions were a family affair occurring intermittently during the period 1895-99. Helly died not at age twenty-six, as Jung claims, but just before her thirtieth birthday, and without unusual deterioration, contrary to Jung's report.[24] Also, judging from the tone of a note from Jung to Helly while they were both in Paris after the period of the

---

21. MDR, 50.

22. Jaffé, *Jung's Last Years*, 3.

23. Among this literature Jung lists authors such as Zoellner, Crookes, Duprel, Eschenmayer, Passavant, Kerner, Görres, and Swedenborg; see *MDR*, 99. Jung compares S.W. in his case report with Kerner's clairvoyant; cf. *CW*1: 49, 59, 73, 116.

24. Stefanie Zumstein-Preiswerk, *Jungs Medium: Die Geschichte der Helly Preiswerk* (Munich: Kindler, 1975). For Jung's report, cf. *MDR*, 107.

seance sessions in Basel, their relationship was mutual and by no means that of a detached scientist and his subject.[25]

What are we to make of these seemingly contradictory accounts of the situation: the scientific, objective account as presented in Jung's dissertation and he more personal, biographical story. By holding to his scientific stance, Jung also holds at a distance the emotional complexities of his maternal (Preiswerk) inheritance. What then happens to the personal factor repressed by the objective attitude?

The refused returns as scandal. Stephanie Zumstein Preiswerk's expose seventy-five years after the event appears with a vengeance to set the record straight. The emotional complexities neglected in Jung's scientific ac count return and claim to be the real facts of the case. The emotion scorned returns as a literalism parallel to that by which it was denied. An avenging subjectivity, by claiming equivalent reality, counters scientific objectivity.

Obviously Zumstein-Preiswerk's expose, which includes Boswellian conversations among persons long dead, is a form of biographical fiction. But is not Jung's scientific mode of telling also a form of fiction? He too has strayed from and misrepresented certain "facts." His pretense of objectivity has occluded his subjective involvement.

We had best view the "objectivity" of Jung's report as a fictional disguise. Taken as such, his failure to admit his involvement in the case becomes not simply an example of oversight, scientific charlatanism, or personal cowardice—of which, from a "neutral" point of view he might fairly be accused. Rather, his duplicity and his awareness of it helps to create the case as fiction.

25. See James Hillman, "Some Early Background to Jung's Ideas," *Spring: An Annual of Archetypal Psychology and Jungian Thought* (1976): 123–36, in which Zumstein-Preiswerk's book is reviewed. Hillman quotes two letters written by Jung to Helene.

On another level, Jung actually believed himself to be a scientist. The intention of his writing was to elucidate, communicate, instruct, and persuade concerning the "facts" of the psyche. Expositionally, the case of S.W. is addressed to a scientific public in order to aid scientific understanding. It is, after all, a medical dissertation.

Jung's writing style betrays both these modes. There is his stated scientific intention characterized by linear logic and reasoned deduction. But there is a second mode or level in which loose chains of association circle his main line of reasoning. In this mode themes are mentioned, then dropped and never developed into conclusions. Allusions, though sometimes grouped, give a sense of the work as itself incomplete, unfinished—as though the psyche itself were incomplete. Momentary themes begin, and end in loose ends. Particulars and side issues stand out strangely. What is frequently most interesting in Jung are these side issues that originate and never fully unfold, themes hinted at which never become thematic.

This fragmentary, effusive style so characteristic of Jung's writing parallels his mediumistic cousin psychologically. S.W.'s psyche was profuse with autonomous personalities.

In the autobiography Jung speaks of his own personalities as No. 1 and No. 2, and parallels this phenomenon with the case of S.W. From her he learned "how a Number 2 personality is formed, how it enters into a child's consciousness and finally integrates it into itself."[26] Then again, "in most cases where a split-off complex manifests itself it does so in the form of a personality, as if the complex had a consciousness of itself...I dealt long ago with this phenomenon of personified complexes in my doctoral dissertation."[27] By recognizing his own dissociability in the

---

26. *MDR*, 107.
27. *MDR*, 322.

autonomous "personalities" of his subject, Jung is able to theorize a multiple basis of independent intentionalities in regard to the psyche in general.

But what of Jung's scientific pose? Insofar as he is aware of it as a posture, aware of his own duplicity, Jung becomes an accomplice in rendering the case report a fictional enterprise. If a fiction, the disguise of the narrator, his persona, becomes important.

There are certain advantages to the disguise that Jung adopts. By pretending he does not know his subject, S.W., Jung creates a mood of facticity, a sense that the events related cannot be questioned outside the scientific terms in which they are presented. In this way his account has a categorical effect. If it is to be countered, it must be within the same genre he has presented. Thus the scientific convention provides Jung a convenient way of exteriorizing, containing, and shaping ideas of personal and more than personal concern.

That Jung was not unaware of this sense of his case as artifact is shown in his autobiography. He admits, "Even now I can do no more than tell stories—'mythologize.'"[28] In recognizing the role of story-telling and mythologizing, Jung effectively reimagines scientific concerns as fictional renderings and dramatic enactments. The case may thus be seen as not so much a detached description of events as a dramatic exposing of them. The insides of a psychological situation are turned outside through enactment. The many "personalities" of a dissociable psyche, of which the scientific persona is only one, are exteriorized as the *dramatis personae* of the case.

S.W. was a fitting medium for this experiment because of her performing talent as an actress. Jung remarks on this ability.

> In her somnambulistic dialogues she copied in a remarkably clever way her dead relatives and acquaintances, with all

---

28. *MDR*, 299.

their foibles, so that she made a lasting impression even on persons not easily influenced. She could also hit off people whom she knew only from hearsay, doing it so well that none of the spectators could deny her at least considerable talent as an actress. Gradually gestures began to accompany the words, and these finally led up to "attitudes passionnelles" and whole dramatic scenes.[29]

In these artistic raptures S.W. moved through and beyond the limits of her conscious, more inhibited personality.

On these occasions she made exclusive use of literary German, which she spoke with perfect ease and assurance, in complete contrast to her usual uncertain and embarrassed manner in the waking state. Her movements were free and of a noble grace, mirroring most beautifully her changing emotions.[30]

Part of Jung's attraction to S.W. and her states was their aesthetic, almost operatic quality. This young cousin had the art of turning Jung's vague intuitions and half-formed intuitions outside into perceptible dramatic states. It was an art that Jung himself lacked. Though he had a tendency to participation mystique, the ability to dissolve his personal boundaries and merge with his surroundings, Jung lacked the ability to shape this merging artistically. In a letter to Aniela Jaffé in 1954 he complains that the artist within him has remained "the merest embryo, incapable of real artistry." He admits a resentment in regard to this lack in his development. "The artist homunculus in me has nourished all sorts of resentments and has obviously taken it very badly that I didn't press the poet's wreath on his head."[31]

---

29. *CW*1: 40.

30. Ibid.

31. C.G. Jung, *Letters*, vol. 2: *1951–1961*, selected and edited by Gerhard Adler in collaboration with Aniela Jaffé; translated by R.F.C. Hull [Princeton, N.J.: Princeton University Press, 1973], 189.

S.W. enacts Jung's aesthetic propensity for him. But he is ambivalent concerning her and her propensity. On the one hand he
is attracted to the uncommonness of her behavior; on the other,
he removes himself from it through scientific abstraction, for he
fears the aesthetic as basically akin to madness. From a distance,
madman and poet appear to Jung interchangeable.

> Persons with habitual hallucinations, and also those who are
> inspired, exhibit these states; they draw the attention of the
> crowd to themselves, now as poets or artists, now as saviors,
> prophets, or founders of new sects.[32]

In speaking of inspiration and hallucination as though they were
interchangeable developments of the same neurotic root, Jung
puts both in question. His ambivalence concern ing the deeper
basis of the psyche, as we saw in the preceding chapter, appears
here in his view of its use as an attention-seeking ruse. What
appears to be art may also be pathology. Throughout his work,
with few notable exceptions, Jung fails to differentiate between
these state. The consequence of this lack of differentiation is
that art remains always somewhat suspect and fearful, and as a
result Jung always feels to some extent justified in his posture of
scientific remove and general abstraction. The multiple, autonomous basis of the psyche is, though inspired, also disreputable
and dangerous.

Jung's "Nietzsche complex" is another manifestation of this
ambivalence in regard to the dangers of creativity. Jung was
drawn to and fascinated by Nietzsche and frequently quoted his
works. But he also feared Nietzsche's fate and insistently warned
that any too deep submersion in the unconscious could result in
the same.

S.W. enacts something of this Nietzschean complex for Jung
in her performances. At one point she warns her brother Albert

---

32. *CW*1: 34.

concerning "N" (Nietzsche): "Albert, Albert, don't you believe
your father? I tell you there are many mistakes in N's teachings."
Then again, "Well then, be frightened; I am. I warn you about N's
teaching."[33]

Later, in a discussion of cryptomnesia, Jung refers explicitly
to Nietzsche as having unconsciously reproduced in *Thus Spake
Zarathustra* a passage from the spiritualistic *Blätter aus Prevorst*
of Justinus Kerner.[34] Jung's point is that a mediation of unconscious images may result in what appears to be plagiarism. This
psychic contagion (*participation mystique*) is both a natural and
yet, for Jung in his scientific stance, a fearful situation, since it
threatens the breakdown of boundaries between events.

Of course it is just this dissolving of boundaries that characterizes Jung's underlying relationship and fascination with S.W.
S.W. picks up and enacts Jung's underlying complexes. Another
example of this contagion appears in S.W.'s dramatization of
Jung's Goethe concerns.[35]

According to family legend, Jung's paternal grand father was
an illegitimate son of Goethe and the actress Sophie Ziegler.
Though this story was never substantiated, it persisted because,
according to Aniela Jaffé, it served to help explain Jung's lifelong
fascination with Goethe.[36]

S.W. in the form of one of her "personalities," Ivenes, substantiated this fantasy in a tale of her reincarnations. At the beginning

---

33. *CW*1: 33.

34. *CW*1: 140ff. *Blätter aus Prevorst* [Leaves from Prevorst], a psychic
periodical, was founded by Kerner in 1831. After publication of twelve volumes, it was superseded in 1839 by *Magikon: Archive für Beobachtungen aus
dem Gebiete der Geisterkunde und des magnetischen und magischen Lebens*
(Magikon; or, Archives for Observations Concerning the Realms of the Spirit World of Magnetic Life).

35. *CW*1: 63.

36. *MDR*, 35–36, 35n.1, 87.

of the nineteenth century she claimed to have been the Clairvoyant of Prevorst, and at the end of the eighteenth century a clergy-
man's wife who had been seduced by Goethe and had borne him
a son.[37]

In addition to these personages, S.W. embodied for Jung many
of his psychological attitudes. Since Jung as narrator of the case
study was in the fictional stance of observer, much of what was to
become manifest as his own psychological attitude had to be spoken by her. For example, to Jung's critical, rational explanations
of her state, S.W. responds:

> I do not know if what the spirits say and teach me is true, nor
> do I know if they really are the people they call themselves;
> but that my spirits exist is beyond question. I see them before
> me, I can touch them. I speak to them about everything I
> wish as naturally as I'm talking to you. They must be real.[38]

Jung, of course, also regards these figures as real, as we saw in
his dialogues with imaginal figures in the previous chapter. Here,
however, the drama is such that he is cast in the role of the critic.
In this stance he informs S.W. that her manifestations are an illness. From this she recoils.

> She felt so hurt by my remarks that she closed up in my
> presence and for a long time refused to experiment if I was
> there; hence I took cannot to express my doubts and mis-
> givings aloud.[39]

Jung silences himself as critical observer, and in doing so also
indirectly comments on the harmfulness of removed judgment.
Judgment from a distance requires generalization of the phenomena. If the psyche consists of multiple personalities, each with its
own intentions and characteristics, then to regard it distantly and

---

37. *CW*1: 63.
38. *CW*1: 43.
39. Ibid.

generally (in this case through diagnosis) undermines its genuinely autonomous nature.

S.W.'s enactions required a suspension of usual beliefs—such as belief in the conventional boundaries between inner and outer, subjective and objective, the imagined and the real. In her performances inner thoughts turned tables; voices from within spoke in the simulated dialects of actual personages from an historical past.

Outer perceptions, though they sometimes played into these visions and hallucinations, did not appear to determine them causally. These psychic enactments displayed an organizing capacity that sometimes appeared to draw from surrounding phenomena but at other times not. The nexus of psychic organization these performances implied was from a realm between inner and outer, participant in both.

This in-between, imagistic realm is an *esse in anima*—a notion we shall return to throughout this thesis, since it is in Jung's thought a basic nexus of imaginal, psychic space. *Esse in anima* is a realm between *intellectus* and *res,* neither explainable factually through reference to the sensate nor derivative of pure ideation. Eventually Jung designates this imagistic realm "psychic reality," accord ing it a reality equal to any other, and specifying it as that realm within which psychology works. The material of this reality is "subtle," and consists of shadows and refractions between the realities of internal and external worlds. Insofar as S.W.'s performances are enactments of this imaginal space and subtle body, she is thus another manifestation of the "esthetic lady" we saw in the previous section. S.W.'s enactments conjure imagistic presences and interworkings, not wholly real in an objective sense, but of an imaginal or psychic reality.

When Jung describes S.W.'s "personalities," his position shifts from objective, scientific distance to a more direct personal engagement, as though he were describing actual persons about whom he had personal feelings. Some of these characters he clearly does not take to—such as "Mr. P.R.," who is commonplace and frivolous, or "the grandfather," who speaks artificially in biblical maxim and verse, or the circumlocutious "Ulrich von Gerbenstein."

Jung's personal judgment in regard to these figures rests on underlying aesthetic evaluations of them. He considers uninteresting those who are flat, banal, or repetitive—like poor characters in a drama. Accordingly when such characters dominate—as von Gerbenstein does increasingly—Jung views the sessions as deteriorating. He describes this deterioration also in aesthetic terms. Toward the end,

> the phenomena lost their plasticity and became ever shallower; characters which at first were well differentiated became by degrees inextricably mixed. The psychological yield grew more and more meagre.[40]

As the aesthetic level of the sessions deteriorated, they became for Jung of less interest psychologically as well. Of most interest to him were thu more surprising and promising figures. One such figure was "Ivenes," whom Jung describes as a more complex and mature personality than the medium. herself. According to him,

> it was in this state [as Ivenes] that [S.W.] achieved her best results, whereas her romances corresponded more closely to her waking interests.[41]

S.W.'s "waking interests" were those of a typically romantic fifteen-and-a-half-year-old. In her normal state S.W. was frivolous, flirtatious and somewhat childish. Jung describes her as indulging herself "with unconcealed pleasure about all her little childish

---

40. *CW*1: 134.
41. *CW*1: 44.

experiences, the flirtations and love secrets, the naughtiness and rudeness of her companions and playmates."[42]

Jung regards Ivenes as a superior figure, and as one whose awareness is more encompassing than all the others. Ivenes is cognizant of waking occurrences, as well as of each of the other somnolent personalities. Since she can remember her visionary states and experiences, she forms a continuity of awareness through the sessions. That Jung should designate an unconscious figure as the most conscious is a radical statement, theoretically, for it implies that the most conscious part of the personality need not be the literal person nor need it be in a waking state. Consciousness can exist as an unconscious, autonomous figure.

When Jung is most engaged with these figures, he views the psyche as possessing its own vitality and means of organization. This psyche does not require structuring from the outside by means of scientific conceptions and frame works but is capable of generating forms of awareness from within itself. These need not be comprehensive or systematic. In fact, systematization can work to their detriment, as shown at one point during the seance sessions.

There is a period toward the end of the series where S.W. turns her attention to the production of an elaborate "power system." This comprehensive cosmic structure included complicated circles of matter and various schematizations of forces of good and evil. Jung marks the production of this system as corresponding to the deterioration of the sessions, since it replaced the "richness and plasticity of form" of the original visions.

After the production of this power system, S.W.'s sensitivities became increasingly stereotypic and repetitive, such that she "was only able to report ecstatic feelings in the presence of good

---

42. Ibid.

spirits and disagreeable ones in that of bad spirits. Nothing new was produced."[43]

As S.W. became more "normal," she lost her aesthetic sensibilities. Her visions became increasingly uninteresting and her personalities appeared contrived. A feeling grew among the participants that she was merely "seeking to make an impression on her audience." S.W. was losing her powers and finally, in an effort to regain them, was caught cheating *in flagrante.* So ended the seance sessions and S.W.'s dramatizations.

Our underlying concern throughout this elaboration has been to trace Jung's shifting positions as narrator and to draw out the implications of these positions for his over all psychological vision.

We find that Jung alternates between two attitudes regarding the psyche's multiplicity. The first attitude so completely accepts the phenomena that present themselves as independent realities that it assumes their existence along with them. The psyche is experienced as it appears—i.e., as multiple, and as though it had consciousnesses and intentionalities of its own. In this manner Jung arrives at a model of the psyche as basically multiple and autonomous, each complex or personality possessing its own aware ness. When using this model, Jung looks to individual complexes—such as Ivenes—to see the particular intentions and forms of making generating from them.

When Jung observes the personalities of s. w. this way he sees them as autonomous. They speak and behave independently in ways S. W. herself does not. Ulrich von Gerbenstein speaks in fluent literary German with a North German accent, whereas S.W. speaks only in rural Swiss dialect. Unlike S.W., her grandfather is

43. *CW*1: 71.

pretentious and artificial. Ivenes is mature and serious. Mr. P.R. is a flirt. A mystical Jewess is responsible for the cosmic system, and so on. The figures are regarded as authentically independent.

The second attitude in Jung is that of the systematic scientist. When taking this stance, he is at an objective remove from the phenomena he is considering. From this remove he assumes the psyche to be basically a unitary system, so that complexes, rather than possessing consciousness in themselves, are "dissociations," or fragmentations of an imagined original unity. Multiplicity is then seen as the result of pathology rather than the basic nature of the psyche itself. From this position of remove, Jung defines complexes as "psychic fragments which have split off owing to traumatic influences or certain incompatible tendencies."[44] In this model complexes are not so much of interest in themselves. What receives priority is that original unity from which they have split.

How Jung regards his fiction corresponds with whether he takes his orientation from a unitary or multiple model of the psyche. When he forgets his subjective stance, thinking it objective and what he observes "factual," we find him then working singularly and unitarily. When he is aware of his fictional stance, of his subjectivity and mythologizing, we find him regarding psychic phenomena as consisting of multiple particulars, each with its own intentionality and potential forms or development.

The distinction between these two views also has implications for the psyche as a formative process. If the psyche is multiple, and its makings proceed variously, then the intentions of these makings are peculiar to each distinct activity, organic within it. Seen in this way each activity has potential form and inherent aim (what Jung later refers to as "purpose" or telos).[45]

---

44. *MDR*, 393.
45. See *CW*8: 456; *CW*4: 452, 490.

If on the other hand the psyche is a unity, whatever work-ings do not fit into the hypostatized form of that unity tend to be seen as aberrant, unfitting, pathological. The situation is similar to that of the mandala mentioned in the previous chapter. When Jung works from an *a priori* system of wholeness, what inter-rupts—whether the voice of an aesthetic lady or an autonomous complex—is viewed as aberrant and usually dismissed.

These two attitudes in Jung, the scientific and the phenom-enological, continue in various permutations through out his work. The task thus becomes seeing in each instance that Jung brings to the fore—the Jung who credits and engages vis-à-vis the phenomena or the Jung who believes himself an observer. In the first case, both Jung and the phenomena he is observing become imaginative entities, involved in imaginative, fictional interwork-ings. In the second, Jung becomes the observer of phenomena he must then categorically place and systematically differentiate.

To what extent is Jung's orientation phenomenal? So far our answer to this question has been that it both is and is not. Insofar as Jung begins with the uniqueness of phenomena, credited as intentional and multiple, engages with them as a craftsman in service of them, encouraging their potential forms and inherent developments—to this extent, Jung works phenomenally. Where Jung is phenomenal in this sense, he provides the basis for a psy-chological aesthetic. In the following chapter we shall continue gathering the basis for this aesthetic.

CHAPTER THREE

The Aesthetically Immediate and the Unconscious

In Jung's dialogues with the inner figures of Salome, Ka and Philemon, and in his explorations of the personalities of S.W., the psyche presents itself as multiple. At this point plurality is not Jung's construction to explain the nature of the psyche, but rather the way the psyche occurs to him. So to follow Jung phenomenally is to begin in multiplicity. This beginning is also an aesthetic, if we take *aisthesis,* of the senses, as grounding in the immediate sensuous details of what presents itself (as the many figures, multiple, autonomous personalities, were presented to Jung). *Aisthesis* implies distinct actualities, leading to descriptions rather than to secondary rationalizations about descriptions.

This aesthetic concreteness should not be confused with the literal or factual pretense of Jung's psychology—his objective or scientific stance. When Jung maintains it, he distances himself from the immediately concrete through his constructions, as though the events he describes were factual and objectively true rather than merely concrete.[1] When factual, Jung also leaves himself out of the picture, forgetting the sensuousness and the fictional nature of the story in which he is engaged.

By now it should be clear that in referring to the aesthetically immediate we are referring to a concreteness similar to that of a poetic description—i.e., a presentational, imaginative immediacy. This aesthetic concreteness is instinct from the

---

1. For a distinction between the literal and the concrete, see my "On Reduction," in *Echo's Subtle Body,* 151–69.

literal, one-dimensional concreteness of fact. Whereas fact may be regarded as "nothing but" what it represents, the poetically concrete is "more than" any singularly determined representation.[2] From an aesthetic point of view fact becomes factitious, no longer literal.

Aesthetic sensuousness is also distinct from imagined serial causes. Theoretical or psychodynamic explanations of events lack the immediacy of more direct descriptions. As we saw in the preceding chapter, when Jung explains the reasons for the psyche's appearance as multiple by theorizing a preexistent unitary wholeness from which the psyche has dissociated, he is no longer directly describing the phenomena but theorizing about them. The effect of this theorizing is to split ideas concerning the experience from the experience itself. Explanations become more important than the actual experience. So in reconstructing a basis for Jung's aesthetics, we must bracket those theories and explanations not of immediate effect in the work itself.

Fundamental to the entire Jungian theoretical endeavor is the notion of the unconscious. This idea need not be considered a categorical, nonphenomenological construct. It may as well be imagined aesthetically.[3]

Jung defines the unconscious (*Unbewusste*) in the negative as that which is "not conscious (*bewusst*), i.e., not related to the ego in any perceptible way.[4] He differentiates the psychological notion of the unconscious from a philosophical, metaphysical one by maintaining that the psychological concept derives "simply and

2. *CW* 6: 814ff.

3. In reimagining the notion of the unconscious, we are in keeping with the procedure evidenced by Robert Romanyshyn, who reconsidered it in terms of the nonreflected; see his *Psychological Life: From Science to Metaphor* (Austin: University of Texas Press, 1982), 93–97.

4. *CW* 6: 837.

solely from experience."[5] It is a reciprocal or "borderline" concept, known only in its relationship with consciousness.

Thus considered, the unconscious has immediate aesthetic implications. Its existence is known through its effects. It is a negation nonetheless effectively present, and known through an experienced quality different from what is called consciousness. Before elaborating further, we need to turn to Freud's fundamental idea of negation.

In his essay "Negation" (1925), Freud argues that to say something is "not" is at once to have it in mind.[6] The psyche pays no attention to whether statements are issued in negative or positive form; in that they are issued, they exist. In the terms of a later psychologist, George Kelly, the mind operates via "constructs."[7] Some of these constructs are expressed as negatives, some as positives. But whether as negatives or positives, differences from or similarities with, each arm of any construct remains as a psychological presence.

To imagine the situation graphically or presentationally: in an image (a painting, say) what exists shows in the painting. There is no "not" that does not actually present itself, and insofar as it does so it is an "is." There is no place for negation as such in a painting. One cannot paint contradiction. One paints whatever one paints, and whatever one paints exists. Absence or negation may be achieved—as for example the feeling of absence in a Zen painting or a De Chirico—but this absence is achieved in the painting.

If we imagine the psyche as an aesthetic work—a painting in process—then any assertion such as Jung's that he is *not* doing art,

---

5. *CW* 6: 837–42.

6. Sigmund Freud, *Collected Papers*. Authorized translation under the supervision of Joan Riviere, 5 vols. (London: The Hogarth Press and the Institute of Psycho-Analysis, 1924–50), 5: 181–85.

7. George A. Kelly, *A Theory of Personality: The Psychology of Personal Constructs* (New York: W.W. Norton, 1963).

is immediately in the work and inseparable from it. Logically, the situation is quite different; Jung's assertion that he is not doing art states that he simply is not. We take his statement at face value as either true or false. From an aesthetic point of view his denial is nonetheless present in the situation. The difference in readings is determined by the perspective with which one approaches Jung's statement—whether one reads it literally or aesthetically.

The difficulty with the Freudian approach in which the negative particle simply drops out is that the contrast accomplished by the negation is lost as well. By simply turning a negative to a positive as though they were identical, the aesthetic effect of the negation, its tension, is dissipated.

In the approach we are proposing let us therefore respect negation as an aesthetic means, a tool to be used. In this way the unconscious (depth psychology's basic negation) maintains its sense of tension and difference from that which is considered more positively present, or conscious.

Jung's psychology rests on these tensions. Most of his major constructs—introversion/extraversion, ego/self, eros/logos, image/instinct, anima/animus, conscious/unconscious, first-half/second-half, ethics/morals, individual/collective, persona/self—are posited oppositionally as contrasts.

This preference for oppositions can also be found in the work of Jung's mentor and chief at Burghölzli, Eugen Bleuler. In "Die negative Suggestibilität: Ein psychologisches Prototyp des Negativismus [The Negative Suggestibility: A Psychological Prototype of Negativism]" (1905), and in "Zur Theorie des schizophrenen Negativismus [On the Theory of Schizophrenic Negativism]" (1909), both articles quoted by Jung, Bleuler speaks of the psyche as basically ambivalent.[8] Contrasts appear so frequently

---

8. See "The Psychology of Dementia Praecox," in *CW*3: 27f.; "A Criticism of Bleuler's Theory of Schizophrenic Negativism," in ibid., pp. 197–202.

in patients' associations (black-white, tall-short) because, according to Bleuler, the psyche tends to set things up in terms of these contraries. Jung notes that in "primitive language" sometimes the same word is used for opposite notions, whereas in more developed languages the two terms tend to be separated in order to slow down action and "force one to weigh the pros and cons."[9]

This notion of the development of language toward contrariety, the splitting of experience into pros and cons, and the consequent emphasis on decision-making rather than immediate action, again assumes a unitary model of the psyche. The idea is that unity preexists as an original undifferentiated state. Civilization, as well as the civilizing process of the individual psyche, develops out of this oneness by way of oppositions. Thought and experience, consciousness itself, splits into negatives and positives for the sake of psychological development.

According to Jung and Bleuler, with any posited term a negation is contrasted automatically. Contrariety is the association "nearest to hand."[10] Bleuler and Jung's concern here has to do with the negativism evident in certain forms of pathology. The "negative suggestibility" of hysterics balances a positive suggestibility (insuperable autosuggestions), and in dementia praecox "negativism" counters command automatism and echopraxia.[11] Jung quotes Janet as showing how this play of contraries is released through *abaissement du niveau mental* and concludes that in the "apperceptive deterioration" of dementia praecox these contrasts become therefore even more evident.[12]

> Hence, on the question of negativism there is no lack of grounds for the hypothesis that this symptom, too, is closely

---

9. *CW*3: 27–29.
10. *CW*3: 28 and n.54.
11. *CW*3: 27.
12. *CW*3: 29.

connected with "apperceptive deterioration." The central
control of the psyche has become so weak that it can neither promote the positive nor inhibit the negative acts, or
vice versa.[13]

This view of pathology as an "apperceptive deterioration" implies
normalcy as the ability to set things up in terms of opposites and
choose between them, suppressing one or another pole of the
ambivalence. What is not normal, and thus an apperceptive deterioration, is the inability to separate and exclude by way of these
negative-positive oppositions.

The perspective on psychopathology expressed here by Jung
and Bleuler leads most obviously to a rational, developmental
mode of therapeutic treatment—what is currently referred to as
"ego psychology"—in which conscious choice, the ability to separate events into alternatives and to determine direction through
the development of "more highly differentiated," rational, decision-making functions, is the model emphasized. We shall return
to the therapeutic implications of this and other models in a
later chapter on psychological practice. Our present concern is
the more basic one of re-imagining this oppositional tendency of
psychiatric thought.

To do so, we must bracket out the notion of rational development as a psychological goal, and division into contradictory opposites as a means toward that goal. We are left with the
psyche's tendency to create alternatives, which Jung describes
as "negative" and "positive." If we regard these alternatives not
as rational either-or exclusions, not as literally negative or positive, we may see Jung's use of them as an aesthetic, psychological means of creating value differences, contrasts. The devalued
or "inhibited act" continues to exist psychologically through its

_____

13. Ibid.

contrast with the act promoted. Psychic development thus considered may be seen as proceeding through the creation of various evaluative contrasts. Such contrasts serve many purposes—to detach foreground from background, to determine emphasis or perspective, and to create line and direction.

Our primary concern here has been to distinguish contradiction from contrast as a mode of negation. Whereas contradiction logocentrically believes itself to have literally excluded what has been negated, negation viewed from the attitude of contrast creates merely a working tension. Aesthetically it is not so much a matter of what the speaker *believes* he has effected with his negation as it is a matter of viewing the negation in terms of its tensions.

The point is not to get rid of negation through making a hidden identity of such statements (as does Freud), dropping out the negative term in order to see it as positive ("I do not love you" as identical with "I love you").[14] Indeed, aesthetically, imagistically they are not identical. They feel different. Though the content "love" is the same in both cases, the quality of the tension in each contrary statement is unique.

From an aesthetic point of view we also cannot simply transcend the problem by saying nihilistically that nothing is, or by way of a spiritualist enlightenment, that all that is is not. An aesthetic point of view is different from each of these in that whatever is expressed in tension must be preserved as essential to meaning, to the work.

Now how does this apply to Jung's statement, "no, it is not art!" It puts us back into the tension with which we began, but now we see the tension as an effect of the aesthetic anima. The tension no longer has to do with. accepting or denying the figure. Rather, the figure bears the aesthetic quality of contrast.

---

14. This example was taken from Freud's "On the Mechanism of Paranoia," in Freud, *Collected Papers,* 3: 448–51.

But how does this aesthetic need for contrast show in the realm of psychological ideas? Certainly it implies that negation need not be taken literally. It also implies that negation, contrast, and the tensions these modes effect, are essential to depth psychology's aesthetic.

An example of the necessity of this tension is close at hand in the ideational interrelationship of Jung and his mentor Bleuler. We mentioned Bleuler's view concerning the ambivalence of psychic phenomena. Jung embraces this view, and in his paper "The Psychology of Dementia Praecox" (1907) extensively quotes Bleuler's ideas, praising them for the understanding they give to negativistic phenomena.[15]

Then the oddity. In 1911 Jung publishes a paper called "A Criticism of Bleuler's Theory of Schizophrenic Negativism" in which he attacks Bleuler's discussion of negativistic causes.[16] Jung maintains that behind each of these causes of negativism is in fact a complex, which complex he at this point interprets in a Freudian manner, so that negativism becomes resistance to a psychosexual content.

What is odd about the pugnacious tone of this article is that Jung's work on the complex was done under the auspices of and in association with Bleuler at Burghölzli. Bleuler was not against the notion of complexes; he helped invent and establish it. Furthermore, the descriptions that Bleuler gives concerning causes of negativism make no radical claims concerning causation, so if Jung were simply concerned with deeper causal explanations, he could merely have added them to Bleuler's descriptions. Bleuler lists negativism, for example, as having to do with the "autistic

---

15. In the foreword Jung states: "My views are not contrivances of a roving fancy, but thoughts which matured in almost daily conversation with my respected chief, Professor Bleuler" (*CW* 3, p. 3).

16. Ibid., pp. 197–202.

withdrawal of the patient into his own fantasies." Jung's objection to this point is that "'autistic withdrawal' into one's fantasies is the same as what I have described elsewhere as the marked proliferation of fantasies relating to the complex. Reinforcement of the complex is identical with increase of resistance."[17]

That Jung should be so adamantly defending psychoanalysis at this point is peculiar, particularly since he was at this time engaged in writing the book that would decisively separate him from Freud—precisely over the psychosexual issue.

We might speculate psychologically that Jung was having personal difficulties with Bleuler, or that he was going through a period in which he felt the need to separate himself from others, particularly from those who had been his superiors.[18] There were probably all sorts of difficulties unknown to us, but since his attack was directed at Bleuler's rather innocuously descriptive list of causes of negativism, perhaps this very descriptiveness was part of the problem. The following is Bleuler's list as quoted by Jung:

> a. Autistic withdrawal of the patient into his own fantasies.
> b. The existence of a "life-wound" (complex) which must be protected from injury.
> c. Misapprehension of the environment and its intentions.
> d. Directly hostile relationship to the environment.
> e. The pathological irritability of schizophrenics.
> f. "Pressure of ideas" and other impediments to thought and action.
> g. "Often sexuality, with its ambivalent feeling-tone, is one of the roots of negativistic reaction."[19]

---

17. *CW*3: 429.

18. For Jung's attempts to separate from Bleuler, see, for example, *The Freud/Jung Letters,* edited by William McGuire, translated by R.F.C. Hull (Princeton, N.J.: Princeton University Press, 1974), 219J, 220J, 222J.

19. *CW*3: 428.

Is it perhaps that these "causes" are too simply descriptive? That is, might it be that the very phenomenology of the descriptions appears to Jung too flaccidly psychiatric and without tension, so that he then creates the tension through his objections? In other words, perhaps Jung's use of strong contrasts, marshaling a causality and a Freudianism that at this point he did not even believe (as we know from *Wandlungen und Symbole der Libido,* a work he was doing at the same time) was to dissipate a phenomenal description that felt to him at this time without tension. If psychology is also an aesthetic, as we are maintaining, then its movement includes the breaking of old forms not wrong in a scientific sense or untrue in a philosophical sense, but which, simply because they are established, must be broken.

This is a further reason why the basic negation, the unconscious, is so very important in depth psychology. It is important because it necessitates a continuous aesthetic movement—a breaking of what was, for the sake of making a further creation. If we regard the unconscious as that which is not known, not yet formed or manifested, and yet effectively present within any work or moment, then an anticipation (thus a movement) is continually generated toward it. The very notion of an unconscious upsets what is, tilts or unbalances a situation from its containment, sets the work dynamically in motion toward something other. The unconscious requires that consciousness be reformed. The aesthetic action of the psyche requires that forms be broken as well as made. It is in this sense that a notion of the unconscious is crucial for understanding an aesthetic of the psyche.

From this point of view it is no accident that Jung's mandala was broken by the aesthetic anima. Jung was, as we remember, drawing daily mandalas in an effort to tie his psychic life together, circumscribing it in the unity of circular containment, when he received via letter the suggestion that his fantasies were related to art. At that moment his mandala broke. This opening and breaking apart of a previous containment is one of the functions of art—which function corresponds with the notion of an active and effectively present unconscious.

CHAPTER FOUR

The Making of a Case Report

We have in the previous chapters gathered a basic ground for Jung's psychological aesthetic. We have seen that it includes immediate, concrete, imaginal presences—his internal figures and S.W.'s psychic "spirits"—and that the dynamics of the making proceeds through contrasts, the most notable of which is that basic negation, the Unconscious. The result of this dynamic, imaginal process is a making in motion, a poiesis in movement.

In psychological making no finished object—such as a painting or a poem—results from the work. The activity of psychology, aptly termed "psychologizing" by James Hillman, is an activity in motion.[1] Verbs and gerunds express it best. Thus the activity of psychology is perhaps more appropriately analogous with arts in their movement, their activity—dan*cing,* ac*ting,* pain*ting,* writ*ing,* sculpt*ing,* film*ing*—than to their finished forms. The analogy breaks down in that all of these other arts may be said to result in something. There is a beginning and an end and a result—a symphony or a performance, something that can be recorded or hung on the wall or presumably performed again. There is a score or script—in short, some evidence that the thing has occurred, some product.

In the activity of psychology there is no resulting product. Even "cure," when presumed as an aim of the activity, is described relatively (relative to the situation) and dynamically. Freud's goals

---

1. James Hillman, *Re-Visioning Psychology* (New York: Harper & Row, 1975), 115.

of love and work are sufficiently vague to escape any precise framing. The same is true of Jung's more mysterious "individuation" as a goal of the psychological process. There is no individuated person as an object to be pointed at as though he or she were the goal, the perfect achievement. The art of psychology is in the activity itself.

In the following pages we will examine this activity. We shall do this by way of a critical look at an early case study of Jung's undertaken during the period in which he was most psychiatric.

Psychological cases are reports after the fact, so that what we will be examining is not the therapeutic process as such but rather the art of Jung's report—his modes, assumptions, and their effects. In focusing on the report or description of psychological events, we must treat the description as the event. Thus we are required to bracket any questions concerning the "facts." We have before us only the report, and the author's ideas as they appear in it and bear upon it. Our primary concern, therefore, is to see how these ideas show up in the presentation of the case and the manner of their usefulness.

The Art of Case Report

Jung was aware of the artfulness required in the reporting of clinical cases. In an early paper, "On Simulated Insanity" (1903), published just after "On the Psychology and Psychopathology of So-Called Occult Phenomena," Jung notes the difficulty of persuasive reporting and states that "literary talent" is necessary to render a case effectively. "On Simulated Insanity" exhibits the clinical context from which these remarks derive.[2]

---

2. First published as "Über Simulation von Geistesstörung," *Journal für Psychologie und Neurologie* 2, no. 3 (1903): 181–201; trans. "On Simulated Insanity," in *CW* 1, pp. 159–87.

When a patient is simulating, he is enacting symptoms calcu-lated to effect a determined result, such as his release from prison and transfer to hospital. By behaving in a way that the patient does not feel is entirely factual, or true of himself, he is operat-ing within an illusionary realm. There is an awareness that he is acting and an awareness in his acting, i.e., a consciousness in the simulation telling him how to be. The border between the two, the simulated and the real, is elusive. This elusiveness, according to Jung, can only be comprehended subjectively by the examiner. The examiner stands in relation to the event as a kind of critic or audience. To communicate his impression, a mere scientific report of the facts does not suffice. He must describe convinc-ingly what is essentially an "artful" act on the part of the patient. This description requires an equally developed artful rendering from the critic. Thus, Jung notes, "it is always a risky business to publish these cases at all, for it requires considerable literary tal-ent to lend an air of plausibility to subjective impressions."[3]

Jung has no illusions about his own literary talent. In a letter written to Aniela Jaffé in 1954, he admits his artistic talent to be "the merest embryo," such that he is "incapable of real artistry."[4] Jung distrusts verbal description, distinguishing it from the actual experience, as in the following:

> On paper the interpretation of a dream may look arbitrary, muddled, and spurious: but the same thing in reality can be a little drama of unsurpassed realism. To *experience* a dream and its interpretation is very different from having a tepid rehash set before you on paper.[5]

Jung's frustration with words, his feeling that without literary skill words cannot capture psychological experience, surfaces in "On Simulated Insanity":

---

3. *CW*1: 301.
4. Jung, *Letters*, 2: 130 (22 October 1954).
5. *CW*7: 199.

> It is an unfortunate fact...that the observer cannot convey
> to the reader all the detailed nuances of the picture—the
> changing facial expression, the attitude, verbal response,
> and so forth. Hence no author need be surprised if the
> reader doubts his cases of simulation or at least finds in
> them something to cavil at.[6]

From a literary point of view, to convey "the detailed nuances of
the picture" requires significant selection and the ability to make
what is imaginatively simulated believable as simulated, rather
than as simply true at face value. Should this rendering fail, the
simulated may be misread either as factual or as simply false.
Simulation, however, is not true or false in an objective sense. It is
true fictively, true in the imaginative sense of the patient's enac-
tion. When a patient pretends to be sick, on one level he perhaps
is (because of the exaggerated lengths he has gone to in appear-
ing so, or because he is within his role more completely or in ways
other than he thinks). In other words, it is the *way* in which the
patient has gone about his pretense, the mode of his rendering,
that is determinative. To discern this state of affairs accurately
calls for aesthetic awareness on the part of the physician, and to
communicate it descriptively demands literary skill.

Though Jung feels himself less than gifted at it, we nonetheless find him in his psychiatric narrations including details that
capture mood beyond merely scientific usefulness. Consider his
description in "A Case of Hysterical Stupor in a Prisoner in Deten-
tion," written around the same time, 1902. The report opens with
an event experienced by his patient while in jail.

> When, on the morning of June 4, 1902, the cell was opened
> at 6:30, the patient was standing "rigid [*steif*]" by the door,
> came up to the maid [*Dienstmädchen*] "entirely rigid [*ganz
> steif*]," and furiously demanded that she should "give back

---

6. *CW* 1: 301.

the money she had stolen from her." She waved away the food that was put before her, remarking that there was "poison in it." She began to rage and shout, flinging herself back and forth [*hin und her*] in the cell, kept on asking for her money, saying that she wanted to see the judge at once, etc. At the calls [*Rufen*] of the maid, the jailer came with his wife and assistant, and together they tried to calm her down. Apparently it was a fairly lively scene. They held her by the hands and (according to the maid) also "shook [*schüttelte*]" the patient.[7]

Details are included, such as the patient standing "rigid" at the door, approaching the maid "entirely rigid," waving away the food that was put before her), flinging herself back and forth around the cell, the jailer coming in response to the maid's calls, accompanied by his wife and an assistant, all of them holding the patient's hands and shaking her in an effort to calm her down. These evocative details of the action add little scientific information but they contribute much to the scene and mood of the case as drama. As "significant details" they add color, a certain humor and reality to the recounting—not inappropriately if the report be understood as a form of rendering.

This form, with its mixture of scientific posture and dramatic event, is characteristic of early psychiatric writing in general. Details of character, behavior, situation, and mood were as important to the telling and as inseparable from the conclusion as are statistical data today. Freud's case studies read with the excitement of detective novels; Bleuler's syndrome examinations make precise and subtle use of detail, forming descriptions that round into moods and shape into characters. The Victorian posture of objectivity was part of the genre. Fact as an "objective entity" was inseparable from the emotional, sometimes florid, situations in

---

7. *CW* 1: 229; translation modified.

which it was embedded. The detached observation that would transform the field into collections of quantifiable results (and relegate depth psychology to the interiority of the *Schreibstube*) had not yet crystallized as a method. This is not to deny the importance of interiority and subjectivity in depth psychological work. They indeed play an important role in Jung's aesthetic, as we shall see in the following section.

An Aesthetics of Subjectivity

Notions of subjectivity, the "subjective factor," "subjective level," and "inner," recur throughout Jung's psychology. In Chapter Two we mention Krafft-Ebing's statement concerning the "subjective character" of psychiatric texts, and Jung's reference to it as explaining why he chose to enter the field of psychiatry. To Jung the statement meant that psychiatric writing was a "subjective confession of the author" turned outward as though objective, backed "with the whole" of the author's experiences and personality. That this objectification of the author's "specific prejudice" and personality structure can be; even must be, turned outward and stand as objective—ennobles the task of psychiatric writing, gives to it a certain daring. This daringness of subjectivity placed outward is art.

By subjectivity Jung does not mean subjectivism. He does not mean an individual viewpoint couched in disclaimers—"I feel," "I think," "from my point of view." He means a more dramatic, bolder art, one which does not shrink from its own inevitable projections. Wolfgang Giegerich speaks of projection as a throwing forth to be followed with the rest of the personality.[8] The emphasis is on a movement outward, which is then to be made manifest, manifested with the whole of the personality behind it, to use Jung's

---

8. "Der Sprung nach dem Wurf," *Gorgo* 1 (1979: 49–71).

phrase. This making, like Olson's projective verse, each instant following instanter, instanter, instanter on the next, leads to a continuous making outward activity, each instance of which subsumes and generates the next.[9]

The source of this generation lies in what Jung calls the subjective or intrapsychic realm. In the introduction to his 1908 paper "The Content of the Psychoses" Jung distinguishes the intrapsychic from the physiological as a basis.[10] When mental behavior is traced to a material first principle, as is the practice of medical science, explanations become sterile, dogmatic and arbitrary. They are sterile in the sense that nothing new results, dogmatic in that they imprison the phenomena smothering it materialistically, and arbitrary in that the particularities of the phenomena are given no credit. Whatever the pattern, it is simply the result of a material disorder, accidental discharges or mistaken patternings of the brain. This scientific approach is like trying to describe the "purpose of a building by a mineralogical analysis of its stones."[11] The pattern or function of the building itself is lost.

Jung's metaphor of the psyche as a building, a functional construction, even in its aberrations or so-called "abnormality," is like the psyche as constant maker, since makings have purpose, reason, functional interconnections. To get to these interconnecting rationalities requires an imaginative subjectivity.

In his studies on association and in his extensive work on dementia praecox, Jung explores this interior realm by imagining

---

9. "And if you also set up as a poet, USE USE USE the process at all points, in any given poem always, always one perception must must must MOVE, INSTANTER, ON ANOTHER!" *Selected Writings of Charles Olson*, edited by Robert Creeley (New York: New Directions, 1966), 17.

10. "Der Inhalt der Psychose," first delivered as an academic lecture, 16 January 1908, trans. in *CW*3, pp. 153–78.

11. *CW*3: 324.

interior associative connections.[12] Verbal patterns that appear disjunctive and meaningless from the outside are condensations, within which are hidden interconnecting, mediate terms. By uncovering these mediate terms within the association, their linkage becomes apparent. For example:

> Q: What is a mammal?
> A: It is a cow, for instance a midwife.

> "Midwife" is an indirect association to "cow" and reveals the probable train of thought: *cow—bears living young—so do human beings—midwife.*[13]

Mediate associations can be imagined such that they form a line of internal connections, making coherent what appears from the outside incomprehensible.

In addition to his association studies Jung tells case stories to illustrate the importance of entering into this subjective realm of understanding. One he elaborates involves a thirty-two-year-old woman who on becoming engaged to be married began to evidence peculiar symptoms. Jung's account goes as follows:

> Once she ornamented her Sunday hat very strikingly with red and green feathers; another time she bought a pair of pince-nez to wear when she went out walking with her fiance. One day the sudden idea that there was something the matter with her teeth would not let her rest, and she decided to get a new set, although it wasn't absolutely necessary. She had all her teeth out under an anaesthetic. The following night she suddenly cried and moaned that she was damned forever, for she had committed a great sin: she should not have allowed her teeth to be extracted. She must be prayed for, so that God would pardon her sin. In vain her friends tried to talk her out of her fears, to assure her that the extraction of teeth was not really a sin; it availed nothing...On the following nights

---

12. Cf. *CW2*; *CW3*, pp. 5–151.
13. *CW3*: 44–45.

the attacks were repeated. On being consulted I found the patient quiet, but with a rather vacant expression. I talked to her about the operation, and she assured me that it was not so dreadful to have teeth extracted, but still it was a great sin, from which position, despite every persuasion, she could net be moved. She continually repeated in plaintive, pathetic tones: "I should not have allowed my teeth to be taken out, yes, yes, it was a great sin and God will never forgive me." She gave the impression of real insanity. A few days later her condition grew worse and she had to be brought to the asylum. The anxiety attack persisted and did not stop it was a disturbance that lasted for months.[14]

Having presented the case, Jung then mimics the usual psychiatric, physiological point of view. Assuming the medical persona, he describes the situation in the following way:

> This is just a typical case of dementia praecox. It is the essence of insanity, of "madness," to talk of nothing but absurdities; the view the diseased mind has of the world is deranged, crazy...The extravagant lamentation about this supposed sin is the result of "inappropriate" emotional emphasis. The eccentric ornamentation of the hat, the pince-nez, are bizarre notions such as are very common in these patients. Somewhere in the brain a few cells have got out of order and produce illogical, senseless ideas of one kind or another which are quite without psychological meaning. The patient is obviously a congenital degenerate with a feeble brain, having from birth a kink which contained the seed of the disorder. For some reason or other the disease suddenly broke out now; it could just as easily have broken out at any other time.[15]

In this caricature of the medical point of view, Jung reveals its underlying attitudes in regard to psychological syndromes. One attitude has to do with typicality. ("This is just a typical case";

---

14. *CW*3: 335.
15. *CW*3: 336.

"bizarre notions...are very common in these patients.") When an event is considered typical its particulars are de-emphasized. Unique symptoms—the feathers, the pince-nez—can be explained away as the "senseless absurdities" typical of madness. Madness is "inappropriate" emotion, the result of "congenital" degeneracy, a kink in the brain at birth. Because of this degeneracy, disordered brain cells give off senseless discharges. These discharges have no relation to situation or context but are accidental and apart.

This kind of psychiatric reading destroys the possibility of fantasy as a *sui qeneris* activity in the psyche. If unusual behavior is meaningless, then by implication only the more usual, that which can be generally understood, appropriated by current rationales, is of value. This medical attitude downplays the psyche as a formative entity, significant even in what appear to be its malformations.

The unusual is, of course, that which is precisely of most interest for questions of psychic generativity. The uncommon reveals the possibility of new combinations, putting things together in ways not to be expected. The condensations Jung finds in what is to normal rationality meaningless word associations show, when looked into more deeply, hidden linkages. The unusual as well as the abnormal have their own logic.

To put it another way, if the psyche is basically dynamic— always involved in making, in constructing, deconstructing of one sort or another—then the reasons for this making can only be known by first crediting the activity as having value. Looked at purposively, the question becomes what is the psyche trying to do? The response to this question is then the fiction of the interpretation.

Jung's particular fiction in regard to the above case of the woman with the pince-nez and feathers is a detective story of sorts in which a secret event once uncovered serves to make sense of the patient's situation. Here is the story in brief.

Years ago the patient had had a lover who had abandoned her but from whom she had conceived a child. She gave birth to the child and had it brought up secretly in the country. Now that she was engaged she was in a dilemma, since she knew that her fiancé would eventually have to learn her secret. Anticipating the humiliation of this disclosure, she attempted to increase her esteem—thus the pince-nez, which she felt engendered respect. Her sin appeared to her foul and ugly, so she adorned herself with feathers in an effort to increase her attractiveness and had her teeth removed in order to replace them with more perfect dentures.

Emotionally and physically exhausted after the operation in which her teeth were removed, she began to have anxiety attacks in her anticipation of the time when her fiance would learn the details of her past. Still unable to admit her secret, she displaced the shame from her secret sin to the "sin" of having her teeth removed.

According to Jung, this behavior was altogether human, "for when we cannot admit a great sin, we deplore a small one with all the greater emphasis."[16]

Jung's manner of unfolding this case (as well presumably as his patient's manner of living it) is a mode of imagining typical of turn of the century depth psychology. The mode assumes a secret "fact" or emotional event, which once uncovered makes rational sense of otherwise bizarre or seemingly meaningless behaviors.

Later Jung will shift his style to a mode that focuses more particularly and symbolically on the details of the behavior, asking questions like, why teeth, why feathers in the hat, why green, and

---

16. *CW*3: 338

why red? What do the pince-nez have to do with "seeing," and so on. He will not be content to rationalize the story in the service of its plot but comes to prefer a less reductive imagining of distinctly psychic (unknown) intentionalities operating relative to the known. Leaving the linear causality of plot, his interpretation will shift toward a more dynamic imagining of energetic compensations and balances.

But here Jung is still in a linear mode of imagining, with the purpose of showing that madness when looked at from the inside is after all not so strange. When subjective motivations and symbolizations are understood, insanity becomes, according to Jung, "simply an unusual reaction to emotional problems which are in no wise foreign to ourselves."[17] The use of plot, with its appeal to rational comprehension, is an outstandingly effective technique to this end.

Also helpful is Jung's rhetorical use of "wir" and "unsere" ("we" and "our") by which he encourages the reader's sympathetic identification with the patient:

> ...we have to feel our way into the psychology of the naive mind. If we have to disclose some painful secret to a person we love, we usually try to strengthen his love beforehand so as to obtain a guarantee of his forgiveness. We do it by flattery or by sulking, or we try to show off the value of our personality so as to raise it in the eyes of the other...And who does not know people who will have their teeth extracted out of sheer vanity, simply in order to wear a denture? After such an operation most people find themselves in a slightly nervous state, when everything becomes more difficult to bear.[18]

The intent of Jung's avuncular, sympathetic (almost condescending) tone is to convince the reader of the inherent reasonableness

---

17. *CW*3: 339.
18. *CW*3: 337.

of the patient's behavior, as though the situation were "just so" and nothing out of the ordinary had occurred.

This technique of normalizing the abnormal can be two edged. On the one hand, it helps to create sympathy for the unusual. On the other, it does so at the expense of the unusual—that is, by making the unusual usual. If reasoned understanding can encompass even the most odd, abnormal, unusual event, then the powers of reason are emphasized and reinforced. Rather than submitting to the odd—an attitude that generally plays the more dominant role in Jung's thinking—the odd is incorporated into what is already known. Thus system encapsulates unique event, the rational co-opts the irrational.

Once again we have arrived at that place in Jung where system encompasses and submerges the unique. This time it is not a mandala that does the work but, though no less pernicious, a systematic normalizing that rationalizes away the odd.

The story that Jung tells to explain his patient's behavior is a trite narrative that fails to do justice to the particular images of her symptomatology: the red and green feathers in her hat, the pince-nez, the removal of her teeth, and the feeling of sin because of this removal. By giving general interpretations to each of these particular images—explaining them as general attempts to increase her attractiveness and respectability, her feeling of sin as a displacement—Jung circumvents a more direct and specifically apt psychological treatment attuned to these particularities, where each image would be regarded as significant in itself. In the same way that a specific image in a poem replaced by another image will alter the effect, even create a different poem, a psychological treatment attuned to its poiesis must respect the components.

Were Jung to focus on the images rather than a narrative reading of the case, we would find him treating each image in turn by amplifying its significance: the hat as a covering of the head as well as its adornment effecting a certain style; feathers as *pars pro toto* birdlike, of the air, a feather in her cap, of the qualities red and green. A symbolic amplification of these colors, along with the patient's associations with them, would lead to specific contrasts in tone and quality of a "red" variety and a "green" variety. He would have focused on the pince-nez as an attempted way of seeing, the removal of teeth as a kind of rite of initiation, including the "sin" of their removal and replacement with false dentures. In each case, the question would be what is the psyche trying to do? What kind of poem with these particular images is the psyche attempting?

As the end of this interpretation one would not get a poem in any formal or literary sense. But one would have a larger imaginative, more reverberative feeling for each of the images, at once particular and impersonal. The implications of Jung's amplificatory method will be explored later. Our purpose here has been only to note briefly a difference between narrative versus imagistic interpretation.

Though Jung's interpretation lacks the more imaginative, sensate, aesthetic focus, it evidences in other respects an aesthetic rationale. We noted the importance of contrast in Jung's psychological method, and return to it now on a more fundamental level.

Statements of Being

"Is" and "is not" are statements of being. From a psychological point of view these statements need not be considered ontologically, but may more appropriately be regarded as strong, foundational forms of contrast. Jung draws on this most basic form of contrast when he posits his view of psychogenic interiority as opposed to the medical view of exterior or physical causation. The medical view is external in that it takes the appearance of bizarre behavior to be what it appears to be. From this exterior position it is assumed that the strangeness of the behavior must be caused by a material disorder. Jung argues against this view. Though bizarre behavior may appear random, as though its material were in disarray, brain cells out of order, this is simply not the case. The truth is that a fiction is being lived internally. This fiction cannot be seen from the outside but only from the inside where the patient's internal, subjective imagining is taking place. This realm is distinctly different from the exterior realm of usual awareness.

In striking this hard, oppositional line between the interior and the exterior, the imaginal and the material, Jung establishes a foundational tension between what "is" versus what "is not" The truth "is" interior and imaginal it "is not" exterior and material.

As we say in Chapter Three, one of the aesthetic implications of the unconscious as a psychological notion is that whatever is explicitly countered is nonetheless present as part of the psychological picture. So we might see Jung's denial of medical materialism as essentially present in his construction, and the strong "is" versus "is not" of this construction as foundationally important to its form. This tension works temporarily because of the caricatured strength of its oppositions, outer versus inner, material versus imagination. It works structurally. Because medical materialism is "not" what Jung is about, it provides the necessary counterforce against which and from which his structure is formed.

Moreover, since Jung's model is meant to balance this counterforce, we can expect it to share some of that model's characteristics, and may be better able to understand why Jung's view of interiority and subjectivity seems so very literal. His account of his patient's fiction must be as rational, though in a different way, as the view he opposes. He must establish a literal interior since his opponent holds to a literal exterior. His interpretation must be as reasonable and logical in its fictional form as the medical is in its physiological form.

An Interplay between the Literal and the Imaginal

In addition to this poiesis of psychological balancing, Jung's method also includes a subtle but continual undercutting of that balance. Jung accomplishes this disbalancing by construing the view he is opposing as more literal than his own. His position then appears the more metaphorical and psychological. In the case we have been considering, the medical position is factual and material. Its view is exterior and most "usual." The interiority, which is Jung's focus, connotes a sense of the hidden, an unknown invisibility that invites imagining, as though an esoteric knowing were possible beyond mere appearance. This illusion of secret knowledge undermines the more apparent and scientifically usual.

In this subversion, the interior, psychological story prevails over the scientific, factual one. We have seen that the psychological acquires strength by becoming as literal in its way as the scientific aims to be. What begins fictionally as an imaginative attempt to capture an interior, psychological story becomes a truth that replaces it. Fiction becomes fact, as though this were the one and only story. Feathers and pince-nez become the ineluctable signs (or tokens) of a bastard child in the country.

Later, in another mood and another moment, Jung will deconstruct this "fact" as well. He will see reductive interpretation—of which this story is an example, in that it reduces symbol to an event located in the past—as inadequate to the nature of symbol, which is "the best possible formulation of a relatively unknown thing."[19] In this mood he will insist upon the polysemous irreducibility of psychic events and their interpretations.

---

19. *CW*6: 814.

This tendency to set up an opposition more literal than the perspective he is offering--whether medical materialism, organicism, Freudianism, Platonism, primitivism, Christianity (all of which he takes on at one point or another)—works only insofar as they *are* more literal than his own position. When they are not, as for example when he focuses on a literary or artistic work (cf. his essays on James Joyce and Pablo Picasso), then Jung must resort to modes of merely comparing or categorizing.

Jung is at his best when engaged in countering more literal positions. Another of his techniques in this regard is to see an underlying theme in the literalism. For beneath this interplay of the factual and the imaginal is an underlying assumption of Jung's concerning the psyche's thematic constancy.

Jung evidences this kind of thinking in "The Content of the Psychoses" in which he discusses historically the changing notions of mental illness.

> The ancient view that every misfortune was the vengeance of offended gods returned in a new guise to suite the times. Just as physical diseases can, in many cases, be traced back to some frivolous self-injury, or sin. Behind this conception, too, lurks the angry deity.[20]

From here Jung proceeds to Pinel's removal of the chains of the insane, the removal of the stigma of criminal, to Esquirol's and Bayle's discoveries of changes in the brain, to the new dogma that mental illness is a disease of the brain. The devil, Jung implies, exists now in the new materialism of the psychiatric viewpoint. The devil has become organic.

By assuming an underlying constancy, the devil, Jung is able to trace it through various historical permutations. The devil exists as fact when in the form of offended god or demon. This

---

20. *CW*3: 321.

fact then becomes mere fantasy when the chains of the insane are removed. The devil then reappears as fact in a new form with the medical organic point of view. In whatever permutation, as fact or fantasy, the devil never ceases to exist. Only the form changes.

The use of a thematic constancy which can then be traced through various phenomena is a favorite technique of Jung's. Behind it is his notion of archetype.

The Archetype as a Poetic Basis

The archetype—which he also calls a "primordial image" (*Urbild* or *urtümliches Bild*)—is a basic principle for Jung. Basic principles provide the ground and potential shape for what is to follow. From a poetic point of view the question is not the philosophical one of whether principles are "true," or the scientific one of adequacy, but in what ways they are imaginatively effective and to what shapes they give rise. Thus a poetic idea is different from an hypothesis. It is not to be proved as fact through the gathering of evidence. So, too, it need not be judged necessarily in terms of its parsimony or clarity or even usefulness as a heuristic device. A psychological idea is adequate insofar as it effectively conjures an imaginative basis for its interworkings and their reverberations.

Jung's basis is imagistic. By calling his primary image "primordial" he gives it priority as culturally first, most basic and ever-present. The primordial never ceases to exist. It is universally existent across cultures, and is the deepest level of, though it preexists, any particular culture. Since this *Urbild* is prior to any other form of experience, image is most basic. Jung's psychology is founded most deeply and ontologically in the realm of image and the imagination.

Jung differentiates what he means by image from the more abstract "idea." An idea may appear a priori and fundamental, but does so because it "derives this quality from its precursor—the primordial, symbolic image."[21] An idea is useful because it is abstract, but this abstraction derives fundamentally from the image. "Its [the idea's] secondary nature as something abstract and derived is a result of the rational elaboration to which the primordial image is subjected to fit it for rational use."[22] An idea is thus a tool derived from a more sensuous, imaginal fundament— i.e., the imagination.

The primordial image is not a form in the Platonic sense, since it is not essentially metaphysical or transcendent. But it is also not derivative of the sensuous or naturalistic world. Thus it cannot be explained by natural or climatic conditions—the rising and setting of the sun, the seasons. It cannot be explained by anything outside of its own formal patterns. Jung speaks of these patterns as the psychic canalizations by which experience is organized. We can see the sun as rising and setting, can experience the seasons as changing because of a psychic possibility, an archetype, enabling this perception. We do not know the rising of the sun as a "fact," we only know a psychological experience of it as behaving in this way.

An archetype is not an inherited idea or representation; it is the possibility for this idea or representation—a patterning of experience, rather than a content as such. It includes instinct and image, behavior and reflection. Jung imagines it as like a spectrum, like the gradations from infrared and ultraviolet.

Since this primordial image or archetype is basically of the imagination, one works with it by way of analogies and images. Thus Jung's definitions of the archetype are analogical: it is like the axial structure of a crystal; it is as though it were an "organ of the pre-rational psyche"; it is like a river bed dug deep with

---

21. *CW*6: 736.
22. Ibid.

cultural experience, a structure of living matter, an image of instinct, the instinct's perception of itself, the source of instincts, the form which instincts assume.[23]

The archetype is a fitting basis for a psychological poiesis, since it invites, even necessitates, this kind of analogical thinking. Psychological making proceeds through a paralleling among events. Jung calls this method "amplification," since each paralleling increases the volume, amplitude, reverberations, the richness of the event being considered.

These parallels are primarily cultural analogues, so that any event being amplified is immediately within a broader cultural base. The implication is that the psyche is not only a biological but also a cultural entity. One is born not like a *tabula rasa*, but within a cultural heritage and a broadly based (universal), cultural context. To be human means to be within the heritage of humanity-its themes and concerns as shown in human works of the imagination, i.e. its folklore, myth, art and so on.

Again it is not that these themes preexist any actual event or experience—they are not inherited ideas—it is that individual experience tends to parallel in its modes and concerns other experiences. Thus we recognize themes, e.g., in art and literature. We recognize them because they make imaginative sense, and because the psyche fundamentally perceives imaginatively, by way of motifs and images.

In the following chapter we shall see how this imagining can be also pathological. Universality does not guarantee normality, as seen in the fact that Jung's early dealing with the archetypes was within pathological contexts. *Wandlungen und Symbole der Libido* (1912), where he first uses the term "primordial image," involves

---

23. *CW* 11: 735; *CW* 15: 127; *CW* 8: 136, 226, 415.

the examination of a series of images of a Miss Miller, images that, according to Jung, led to her final schizophrenic breakdown.[24] The case we will be considering here predates Miller's by at least four years. Though written before Jung had formulated his notion of the primordial image, it shows a recognition of the psyche's imagistic modes of dealing with itself, even in its pathology.

---

24. *Symbols of Transformation* is subtitled "An Analysis of the Prelude to a Case of Schizophrenia."

CHAPTER FIVE

An Aesthetic Syndrome

T he case we are to consider shares features with the case of the woman with pince-nez and feathers discussed in the previous chapter. Both are reported in Jung's essay "Der Inhalt der Psychose" for the purpose of demonstrating that psychosis does indeed have a content, and that this content shows a meaningfulness contrary to medical materialist reductivism. In both case studies it is important for Jung to show a "secret" hidden in the subjectivity of his patients, a plot not apparent in the superficial level of their behaviors.

The case to be reported here differs from the other in that the secret does not end with the revealing of the event that "caused" it, but is continued by a feeling of longing beyond the event. This movement beyond the causality of story necessitates an interpretation that does not stop with the revelation of subjective imaginings. As if in recognition of this new requirement, Jung interrupts his report to make explicit references to the poetic. These do not effect a lasting cure for his patient, and do not solve the problem of psychological report. But they do reveal Jung's difficulty with the poetic.

The Case

Jung describes his subject as a thirty to forty-year-old man,

> a foreign archaeologist of great learning and extraordinary intelligence. He was an intellectually precocious boy, very sensitive, with excellent qualities of character and unusual gifts. Physically he was small, weakly, and afflicted with a stammer. Brought up and educated abroad, he afterwards studied for several terms in B. Up to this point there had

been no disturbances of any kind. On completing his university studies he immersed himself in his archeological work, which gradually absorbed him to such an extent that he was dead to the world and all its pleasures. He worked incessantly, and buried himself entirely in his books. He became thoroughly unsociable; awkward and shy in society before, he now shunned it altogether, and saw no one beyond a few friends. He thus led the life of a hermit devoted entirely to science.

A few years later, on a holiday tour, he revisited B., where he remained a few days...The few acquaintances he had there found him strange, taciturn, and nervous...Soon afterwards a peculiar state of excitement supervened, which rapidly passed over into frenzy. He was brought to the asylum...He gradually became quieter, and one day he came to himself as if waking out of a long, confused dream...He returned home and again immersed himself in his books. In the following years he published several outstanding works, but, as before, his life was that of a hermit living entirely in his books and dead to the world. Gradually he got the reputation of being a dried-up misanthropist, with no feeling or the beauty of life.

A few years after his first illness a short holiday trip again brought him to B....One day he was suddenly overcome by a feeling of faintness and lay down in the street. He was carried into a neighboring house, where he immediately became violently excited. He began to perform gymnastics, jumped over the rails of the bed, turned somersaults in the room, started declaiming in a loud voice, sang improvised poems, etc. Again he was brought to the asylum. The excitement continued. He extolled his wonderful muscles, his beautiful figure, his enormous strength. He believed he had discovered a law of nature by which a marvellous voice could be developed. He regarded himself as a great singer and a unique orator, and at the same time he was a divinely inspired poet and composer to whom the verse came simultaneously with the melody.[1]

---

1. *CW*3: 341–43.

As key to this case Jung again uncovers an interior reality. This time the secret plot has to do with the patient's frustrated love and unfulfilled longings. The story goes as follows:

> When our patient was a student he learnt to know and love a girl student. Together they took many solitary walks in the environs of the town, but his exceeding timidity and bashfulness (the lot of the stammerer) never allowed him an opportunity to get out the appropriate words. Moreover he was poor and had nothing to offer her but hopes. The time came for the termination of his studies; she went away, and he also, and they never saw one another again. And not long afterwards he heard she had married someone else. Then he relinquished his hopes, but he did not know that Eros never emancipates his slaves.
>
> He buried himself in abstract learning, not to forget, but to work for her in his thoughts. He wanted to keep the love in his heart quite secret, and never to betray that secret. He would dedicate his works to her without her ever knowing it. The compromise succeeded, but not for long.[2]

In addition to this interior story, Jung draws upon the dynamic notions of wish-fulfillment and compensation to explain his case. The patient's delusional fantasies of beauty, strength, and poetic inspiration are in this view attempts to make up for the opportunity he missed.

> We can see that these contrasts, the so-called delusions of grandeur, are very subtly attuned to the deficiencies in the patient's personality. They are deficiencies which any one of us would certainly feel as a lack. Who has not felt the need to console himself for the aridity of his profession and of his life with the joys of poetry and music, and to restore to his body the natural strength and beauty stolen from it by the atmosphere of the study? Finally, who does not recall with envy the energy of Demosthenes who, despite his stammer,

---

2. *CW*3: 349–50.

became a great orator? If our patient filled the obvious gaps in his physical and psychic life by delusionally fulfilled wishes, we may also conjecture that those soft love-songs which he sang from time to time filled a painful blank in his being, making up for a lack which became the more agonizing the more it was concealed.[3]

In the above passage Jung uses the psychodynamic notions of compensation and wish-fulfillment to explain his patient's delusional enactments and feelings of grandeur. In so doing, Jung moves from the linear causality of a story to the energetic causality of psychodynamics. He argues as before by means of a rhetorical appeal to common experience ("Who has not felt the need to console himself") and is careful to frame his interpretation hypothetically, as conjecture ("If...we may also conjecture..."). Psychodynamic elaborations such as these can be helpful insofar as they break up the "just so" sequential causality implied in storytelling. By adding to the story another level or dynamic, the story changes so that it is no longer determined simply by the sequence of event. Psychodynamic interpretation can bring to the story a certain richness of levels and possibilities. But it can also present new difficulties. If these interpretations are not handled simply as stories (fictions) in themselves, they become instead rigidified conceptions that replace the original story.

Compensation and wish-fulfillment, the mechanisms Jung assumes in the above interpretation, are essentially conservative in that they tend to explain events in terms already known—in this case, in terms of those "deficiencies which any one of us would certainly feel as a lack." Furthermore the prior term, that which compensation compensates and the wish fulfills, is regarded as more "real" or more important than the actual event,

---

3. *CW3*: 347.

behavior, symptom being enacted. If our patient's antics are regarded as merely compensatory to a more genuine desire for an actual woman he had known, and his real lack and inability in regard to her, then these aesthetic enactments lose their particular value.

To suggest as we do that this patient's aesthetic attempts are valuable in themselves is by no means to say that they are accomplishments in an artistic sense. In fact, part of their peculiarity is that they are not the achievements the patient supposes. According to Jung the man was "unmusical," his voice was squeaky," "he sang out of tune," and "he was a bad speaker."[4] From a psychological point of view to take these enactments seriously means to stress their value in terms of what they are attempting. Jung speaks of this as a "purposive," "constructive," rather than causally reductive point of view.[5]

To put it another way, we might ask why these particular symptoms? If the patient's aesthetic attempts were merely to attain the attentions of his loved one, why did he not seek to accumulate wealth (which he also lacked), or attempt in some other way to increase his esteem and attractiveness? Why not pince-nez and feathers?

Our quarrel here with the reductiveness of compensation anticipates Jung. In 1916 he redefines what he means by the notion, extending its sense beyond that used by Freud to include a "complementarity." In this definition compensation refers to a filling out or an extension of something as well as to making up for its lack.[6]

---

4. *CW*3: 344.
5. For an example of Jung's use of constructive interpretation, see *CW*7: 132ff.
6. See *CW*8: 489ff.

But even here, in his 1908 text, Jung perhaps senses the limitations of his reductive interpretation, for we find him suddenly breaking off his discussion of the patient's compensatory dynamics and turning instead to a description of the patient's fantasies during his first internment.

This shift in which he puts aside interpretation and explanation is not uncharacteristic. As we saw in Chapter One, there were long periods in his personal development when he gave up trying to interpret what was happening and turned instead to the activity of building, or painting, or sculpting, and he describes his period of analytical disorientation, before he was sure of his own methods, as one in which he "simply letting the patient talk."[7] These moments when Jung puts aside his interpretive methodologies and moves closer to the phenomena open the way to new developments. In the case we are considering, what develops is a detailed, heroic fantasy. Jung describes his patient's fantasy as follows:

> When he [the patient] fell ill he suddenly left the orderly world and found himself in the chaos of an overmastering dream: a sea of blood and fire, the world was out of joint, everywhere conflagrations, volcanic outbursts, earthquakes, mountains caved in, then came tremendous battles in which nation was hurled on nation, more and more he found himself involved in the struggle of nature, he was in the midst of the fighters, wrestling, defending himself, enduring unutterable misery and pain, but gradually exalted and strengthened by a strange, soothing feeling that someone was watching his struggles—that his loved one saw all this from afar. (That was the time when he showed real violence towards his attendants.) He felt his strength increasing and saw himself at the head of great armies which he would lead to victory. Then more battles, and victory at last. As the victor's prize he

7. *CW*4: 532.

> gained his loved one. As he drew near her the illness ceased,
> and he awoke from a long dream.[8]

Through this detailed account of his patient's heroic fantasies, Jung attempts to preserve the actual, imagistic particularities of the experience. This recounting goes beyond a tale of past events as causally responsible for the situation of the present. Rather, there are actual images, in the form of a heroic narrative shown to have occurred in the psychosis itself. Jung also foregoes the usual psychiatric procedure. Rather than sift through to condense the account into the secondary elaboration of a psychiatric description with psychodynamic explanations, Jung repeats particular images from the experience. In refusing to interpret at this point, Jung displays an attitude in keeping with his notion of the priority of imagination and of "symbol…as its own best interpretation."[9]

The fantasy drama of this first episode, from which the patient awakened as if "out of a long, confused dream," evidently "cured" him. Discharged from the hospital he returned to his normal life and was intellectually productive, until once again he returned on holiday to the town of B. His psychosis reappeared, this time in the form of the delusional aesthetic notions that he was an inspired poet, orator, singer, composer, and perfect physical specimen.

Jung situates these aesthetic symptoms as "corresponding to the period of victory in the first psychosis," and designates the point from which the patient's poetry was generated as that place where in his fantasy he drew near to his beloved. The patient describes his emotion at this time as characterized by a "dreamy feeling, as if he stood on the border between two

----

8. *CW*3: 352.
9. *CW*6: 814ff.

different worlds and did not know whether reality was on the right or the left."[10]

This experience of being between realities is the experience of *esse in anima*.[11] Earlier we referred to this realm as a nexus of the psyche's organization. Jung describes *esse in anima* as "a third, mediating standpoint" between *esse in intellectu* and *esse in re*. In this realm between idea and thing, the psyche creates reality. It does so by "continually creative" acts, which are neither literally sensate nor ideational.

> This autonomous activity of the psyche, which can be explained neither as a reflex action to sensory stimuli nor as the executive organ of eternal ideas, is, like every vital process, a continually creative act. The psyche creates reality every day.[12]

Jung regards fantasy as the key to this creative act:

> Fantasy, therefore, seems to me the clearest expression of the specific activity of the psyche...Fantasy it was and ever is which fashions the bridge between the irreconcilable claims of subject and object, introversion and extraversion. In fantasy alone both mechanisms are united.[13]

Once again Jung has arrived at a basis in the imagination. His path has proceeded by way of the subjective imaginings of his patient, through his patient's longings, beyond the explanations of plot or psychodynamics, through the particularities of his patient's report, to an experience on the border between worlds, which is like being, as he puts it elsewhere, on "the rim of the world, where its mirror-image begins."[14] This realm of reflection

---

10. *CW*3: 353.
11. *CW*6: 77.
12. *CW*6: 78.
13. Ibid.
14. *CW*6: 281.

between realities is the place of anima, and so it is here that our patient meets his loved one, and his strange poetry and delusional music begins.

In Chapter One we spoke of anima as both a feminine figure and a general notion for Jung. It is this reflective quality between irreconcilables that mediates to the unconscious. Anima brings with it a sense of illusiveness as well as attachment and closeness. It appears as a real woman (the beloved of our archeologist), immediate, physically real, entangling as though the actual woman, and yet carries an inspirational quality that is more than real and beyond the actuality of the concrete woman wished for.

Returning to our patient in this reflective light, we may see his longing as a longing beyond any actual woman, or any literal event. The woman of his memories serves as a focus and an embodiment for his fantasies. She is, in this sense; the *femme inspiratrice* of his imaginal psychic life, the one for whom he performs.

As an image of the inspiring but unattainable woman, she is indeed behind our patient's actions and is their secret cause. But she is behind them imaginally. Rather than an actual object to be wooed and won, she is the *causa finalis* of his imaginations. In a sense she is the imagination itself, which is why there is no question for our patient of literally attaining her—she is already married, he says. The denouement of his fantasy is the moment of drawing close to her and thus entering the anima's realm of "mirrored realities."

In this realm on the border between realities, the usual boundaries between inner and outer, fantasy and fact, dissolve as our patient described it he "did not know whether reality was on the right or the left." From this midpoint in the imagination, this "third" of psychic reality, life becomes essentially imaginative. Interior and exterior become poetically intermingled. From a position of *esse in anima* there is no question of a literal interior (in the case of our patient, the private interiority of his fantasies) as over against a literal exteriority (the surroundings from which he secluded himself). We shall discuss in Chapter Nine the pathology of this attempted division. For the moment it is enough to say that our patient's problems come not from his entrance into the realm of *esse in anima* but from his attempts to divide himself from it, so that it could be enacted only in his madness. Jung's view of the prognosis is pessimistic. As the patient is released from his second internment, Jung describes the situation as follows:

> Thus the door of the underworld gradually closed. There remained nothing but a certain tenseness of expression, and a look which, though fixed on the outer world, was at the same time turned inwards; and this alone hinted at the silent activity of the unconscious, preparing new solutions for his insoluble problem. Such is the so-called cure in dementia praecox.[15]

Immediately following this passage, Jung turns not to further elaboration regarding the nature of the psychosis as might have been expected, but to a reflection on poetic description:

> Hitherto we psychiatrists were unable to suppress a smile when we read of a poet's attempts to describe a psychosis. These attempts have generally been regarded as quite use-less, on the ground that a poet introduces into his concep-tion of psychosis psychological relationships that are quite foreign to the clinical picture of the disease. But if the poet has not actually set out to copy a case from a text-book of psychiatry he usually knows better than the psychiatrist.[16]

Jung abruptly shifts from his concern with the irresoluble nature of his patient's pathology to a formal passage concern-ing the superiority of poetic over psychiatric description. In this

---

15. *CW*3: 353.
16. *CW*3: 354.

textual shift a strange hiatus is created. Why is it suddenly so important that Jung interrupt his description and, as it were, address the poetic frontally?

There are other places in which Jung declares his alliance with the poetic over the scientific. That in itself is not so unusual. In "Psychology and Literature" (1930), he speaks of the unconscious as being of such a nature that it cannot be understood and interpreted rationally:

> The creative urge which finds its clearest expression in art is irrational and will in the end make a mock of all our rationalistic undertakings. All conscious psychic processes may well be causally explicable; but the creative act, being rooted in the immensity of the unconscious, will forever elude our attempts at understanding. It describes itself only in its manifestations.[17]

The manifestations, which appeared as the images in our patient's fantasies and as the bizarre enactments in his behavior, were evidences of this creative level of the psyche. We have seen that the longings of this patient were longings beyond the possibilities of literal fulfilment, that they were longings in effect for imagination, beauty, poetry, i.e., for *esse in anima.* Because of the nature of this imaginal longing a psychiatric, reductive interpretation of the case is inadequate. A more appropriate treatment requires as basis the priority of image and the imagination. Jung's treatment assumes this insofar as he has presented the patient's images in their descriptive particularity and has not interfered with these images by interpreting them psychiatrically in ways which would lose their imaginal, anima-like quality. The patient arrived through his fantasy enactments at a position of imaginal reality and thus was temporarily cured. But where has Jung arrived? Evidently he, too, has been affected. In

---

17. *CW* 15: 1325.

shifting from his description of the events to a flatfooted attestation to the superiority of poetry, hence opting for the direct presentation of image, Jung creates a hiatus. The positions on either side—description versus presentation, the psychiatric versus the poetic—are through the hiatus strangely suspended.

We have noted Jung· conflicting attitudes throughout his career, the scientific versus the phenomenological, the rational versus the aesthetic, the systematic, generalized versus the particularized, where direct, immediate experience is most prized. In the hiatus of the text these oppositions are temporarily dissolved. This dissolution is *esse in anima.* In other words, it is within the disjuncture of Jung's text, in its absence, that his psychopoetic reality begins.

But simply paying homage to the poet does not solve the problem. Though Jung, as we have seen, makes repeated gestures toward the poetic (by adhering to description without interpretation and emphasizing particularity), he is nonetheless essentially divided. He will never elaborate the psychopoetics toward which his method and many of his insights point. He will remain divided between his scientific and imaginal sympathies, frequently testifying to the latter without allowing it thoroughly to influence his psychology. In the following chapter we explore his attitudes regarding image, perspective, and type for ways in which they contribute to a psychopoetics.

CHAPTER SIX

The Image

In *esse in anima,* the realm to which Jung was carried by his delusional archeologist, conceptual categories dissolve and poetic reality begins. Since *esse in anima* is a midpoint between subjective and objective, imaginative and material, inner and outer, fantasy and reality, it shares something of the nature of each but in a new nonliteral form, which Jung calls "images." Images are the vehicles of psychological reality. As the means by which the psyche renders meaning and experience, the image is basic to a psychopoetics. Jung says that by image he

> does not mean the psychic reflection of an external object, but a concept derived from poetic usage, namely, a figure of fancy or *fantasy-image,* which is related only indirectly to the perception of an external object.[1]

Jung goes on to distinguish between image and hallucination. "The image has the psychological character of a fantasy idea and never the quasi-real character of an hallucination."[2] Image in other words is not perceptual as is an hallucination, but it has a reality of another sort, which Jung calls "psychic reality."[3] The image has boundaries as an entity.

> The inner image is a complex structure made up of the most varied sources. It is no conglomerate, however, but a homogenous product with a meaning of its own. The image is a condensed expression of the psychic situation as a whole, and

---

1. *CW* 6: 743.
2. Ibid.
3. See above, Chapter One, note 20.

not merely, nor even predominantly, of unconscious contents pure and simple.[4]

Image is a condensation of inner subjective, as well as outer sensuous reality:

> The primordial image is thus a condensation of the living process: It gives a co-ordinating and coherent meaning both to sensuous and to inner perceptions, which at first appear without order or connection, and in this way frees psychic energy from its bondage to sheer uncomprehended perception.[5]

The image is, in other words, the psychic principle by which experience is ordered. This view of psychic order implies an ordering by means of imagistic clusters of associative groupings, similar to Jung's theory in his association studies, rather than through a systematic delineating of mental operations. This ordering through multiple clusters also explains why the notion of image for Jung is prior to conceptual ideation and is its source.[6] Though an image has not the clarity of a formed idea, it is the source of vitality beneath ideas. Jung speaks of it in this role as "a self-activating organism, 'endowed with generative power.'" The image "creates reality."[7]

The image is a dynamic entity that identifies the flow of psychic libido between conscious and unconscious as a direct presentation ("the direct expression of psychic life"), and it is also the means by which experience is apprehended.[8] Image "represents the practical formula without which the apprehension of a new situation would be impossible."[9]

---

4. *CW* 6: 745.
5. *CW* 6: 749.
6. *CW* 6: 750.
7. *CW* 6: 78.
8. *CW* 6: 722.
9. *CW* 6: 754

With these characteristics of imaginative generation, immediacy, and perceptual formation we might expect Jung's notion of
image to found his psychology unequivocally on a psychopoetic
basis within a realm of imagination and fantasy. This is not the
case. Even within his descriptions of image we find Jung resort-
ing to his old habits of oppositionalism, as in the following:

> Although, as a rule, no reality-value attaches to the image,
> this can at times actually increase its importance for psychic
> life, since it then has a greater *psychological* value, represent-
> ing an inner reality which often far outweighs the impor-
> tance of external reality. In this case the *orientation*...of the
> individual is concerned less with adaptation to reality than
> with adaptation to inner demands.[10]

In describing image as having "psychological value," as distinct
from "reality value," of "representing an inner reality which often
far outweighs the importance of external reality," Jung again
sets up a division between inner and outer in which the outer
is regarded as merely external and the inner of special value.
Because of this valuation, individual orientation is understand-
ably more concerned with an "adaptation of inner demands."

Jung sometimes uses this division between interior and exterior reality to advantage—as we saw when he sets up the external,
medical materialistic perspective that he then contrasts with an
equally powerful interior story. But here, from a position of *esse
in anima* in which literal boundaries dissolve, the distinction is
unnecessary. Worse, it thrusts us back in a position before the
anima, or the imaginal, was realized.

Again we are troubled by Jung's two attitudes. One attitude
views image as a complex, self-organizing whole, participating in
both interior and exterior realms. Here image is a "direct expression of psychic life," from which we are given the location and

---

10. *CW* 6: 744.

the grounding for an imaginal approach to the psyche. From this basis one could proceed, were it not that once again Jung's dichotomous attitude interferes by stressing the very division, interior and exterior, that the notion of image was meant to unite. It is as if Jung has not fully located himself within the realization at which he has arrived. The space of imaginal reality, the aesthetic, *esse in anima,* has been seen and recognized but is still denied.

One of the ways this denial occurs in Jung is in his tendency to move from the description of the image to a distancing in which he makes prescriptions concerning it. In the following passage Jung describes the composition of image, then in a final sentence distances himself and, again assuming an opposition, dictates the manner by which interpretation is to proceed.

> The inner image is a complex structure made up of the most varied material from the most varied sources. It is no conglomerate, however, but a homogenous product with a meaning of its own. The image is a *condensed expression of the psychic situation as a whole,* and not merely, nor predominately of unconscious contents pure and simple. It undoubtedly does express unconscious contents, but not the whole of them, only those that are momentarily constellated. This constellation is the result of the spontaneous activity on the one hand and of the momentary conscious situation on the other, which always stimulates the activity of relevant subliminal material and at the same time inhibits their relevant. Accordingly the image is an expression of the unconscious as well as the conscious situation of the moment. The interpretation of its meaning, therefore, can start neither from the conscious alone nor from the unconscious alone, but only from their reciprocal relationship.[11]

If the image is an "expression of the unconscious as well as the conscious situation of the moment," then interpretation of it

---

11. *CW* 6: 745.

would *necessarily* issue from both at once. For Jung to state that interpretation starts "neither from the conscious alone nor from the unconscious alone" implies that somehow he still regards them as essentially separate.

The effect of this program in the act of interpreting is to lead one to consider first the conscious situation and then the unconscious as different events. One ends up working not from an *esse in anima* but a bipolar model, attending first to one side then to the other as though they were different realities. Prescriptions imply a lack of trust that psychic phenomena—in this case, esse in anima—will issue in action and praxis. Jung's distrust hides also a prejudice in regard to the internality of events, which seems to him in conflict with their externality. He speaks of inner reality as having "greater psychological value," a value that "often far outweighs the importance of external reality."[12]

External reality tended to be positivistic for Jung, as we saw in Chapter Four, and representative of the materialistic views of traditional psychiatry. Therefore Jung is in the position of having to reclaim an externality he has hitherto, both personally and theoretically, regarded as a rival position.

In this light, Jung's prescription may be seen as an attempt to supplement his own characterological, methodological leanings. But his terms do not really change. Though the image is a "condensed expression of the psychic situation as a whole," the two sides of that whole—the unconscious interior and the conscious exterior—stay fixed and defined; their positions are unlikely to transpose. Unconsciousness is inside; consciousness works outside. The one is psychological reality and the other external reality.

From a position of *esse in anima,* image and the imagination invite more potentially fruitful distinctions than those of interior

---

12. *CW* 6: 744.

and exterior, unconscious versus conscious. Of more value, for example, might be a distinction between the literal and the concrete—since these are attitudes toward rather than categorical distinctions of phenomena. Let us say that the literal interpretation characterizes an event seen singularly as "only such," "nothing but" whereas the concrete one regards the event as sensuous, "substantial," and embodied, though not necessarily one-dimensionally literal. An image is, in terms of this distinction, concrete but not literal. The advantage of this distinction between the literal and the concrete is that it applies to both "inner" and "outer" realms of experience, i.e., it does not presuppose a divided world.

Distinctions such as these might have helped Jung in working with the psyche from a more imaginative base. But since he is not fully within the ground to which his insights have led, he ends up by failing to explore alternative modes for working with it. He has intuited the realm of anima, but his conceptual models will not let him stay with it or in it.

The distinctions Jung does make with regard to images are generally of a more philosophical, abstract nature. He distinguishes, for example, between the "virtual" or *a priori* image and the manifest or "actual" image. The virtual image corresponds with his notion of the archetype per , and its actual manifestation corresponds with what he terms the "archetypal image."[13] The virtual image is unknowable as such, merely a potentiality. According to this idea, the image itself cannot be seen; it can only be inferred from its manifestation, the actual image.

The distinction between the virtual and the actual, which Jung refers to repeatedly, is of little relevance to the development of a psychopoetics. One might imagine a psychopoetic interpreter as primarily concerned with the manifest, the direct presentation

---

13. *CW*7: 300.

of the image as phenomenally immediate. This is in keeping with Jung's definition of the image as a "direct expression of psychic life"; whereas his distinction about the state of affairs before the event, in which there exists an archetype *per se,* leads one into reflections of a more philosophical sort.

Also problematic are Jung's distinctions between personal and primordial images (which parallel those of the personal and collective unconscious). By personal images Jung meant images reflecting an individual's unique history, circumstances, and environment—a person's individual family, faces known to him, places, and so on. Personal images, such as those occurring in what Jung calls "small dreams," are images that would not be recognized by persons other than the dreamer (apart from those who share the same personal concerns) as important and meaningful.[14]

Of more importance for Jung were those images he termed "primordial" and which he saw as occurring in "big dreams." In calling these images primordial, Jung meant to point out their larger, more collective qualities. Such images structure individual elements (presumably personal images) in uncanny ways, lending them mythological or archaic qualities and an emotional affect all out of proportion with merely personal significance. Because of their collective nature, primordial images bring the individual into contact with meanings and patterns of experience of more general concern, thus leading the individual out of isolation as a separate entity and into a community. This contact Jung sees as a fundamental purpose of the primordial image.[15]

In his essay "Psychology and Literature," in which Jung discusses psychological interpretation in regard to literary texts, he links up personal images deriving from the personal unconscious with the "psychological novel" as distinct from the more

---

14. See *CW*3: 524ff.
15. *CW*13: 396.

profound "visionary · texts. By psychological works he means those concerned with "man's conscious life—with crucial experiences, powerful emotions, suffering, passion, the stuff of human fate in general." In his view "no obscurity surrounds [these works], for they fully explain themselves in their own terms."[16] Presumably, if these personal works are to be interpreted at all, they will be read reductively—since causal, reductive treatments are best suited to personal psychology.[17] Visionary works, however, go beyond human passion and express "a more than personal destiny"[18] They point toward the unknown, "unfathomable abyss of the unborn and of things yet to be" and are best treated symbolically (which, for Jung, means non-reductively).[19]

With this categorical distinction between the personal and the primordial, Jung denies the personal the possibility of symbolic treatment, so that it is condemned to remain on a merely personal, naturalistic, literal level. Images are no longer images at all, according to Jung's definition, but signs pointing to thoroughly personal referents.[20]

The images of visionary literature, on the contrary, are regarded as highly symbolic and as pointing to mythical meanings beyond themselves. In itself this primordial experience is "wordless and imageless," for it is a vision seen "as in a glass darkly."[21] Jung's emphasis here is not on image as such but on

16. *CW*15: 139.

17. In this personal realm, according to Jung, "Even the psychic raw material, the experiences themselves, have nothing strange about them; on the contrary, they have been known from the beginning of time—passion and its fated outcome, human destiny and its sufferings, eternal nature with its beauty and horror" (*CW*15: 140).

18. *CW*15: 148.

19. *CW*15: 141.

20. Cf. sign versus symbol, *CW*5: 114, 180, 329; *CW*6: 201, 788, 814; *CW*7: 492; *CW*8: 88, 644; *CW*9.2: 127; *CW*15: 105; *CW*16: 339, 362; *CW*18: 482.

21. *CW*15: 151.

meanings beyond image, meanings so pure that they can only be intuited. With this visionary view the sensuousness of image as an *esse in anima* is left in the dust. The visionary insists on such an ultimate purity of experience that the phenomenal is relegated to a secondary level of reality.

The result of Jung's categorical distinction between personal and visionary art is that there is no longer a place for image as central in either the personal or the visionary. The personal loses the possibility for a more than personal, symbolic understanding, and the visionary is inflated beyond concrete actuality. This apotheosis of the visionary into myth and meaning tends also to group images into more general categories. Images become merely examples of the Earth Mother, the Trickster, the Wise Old Man, and so on. The particular image gets engulfed by more general archetypal thematics.

So, too, the particular means by which an artist renders a work—his use of language, form, technique—becomes less important for the interpretation than the capturing of the general meaning toward which the work points. As a result, that which makes art an art rather than something else (a philosophical statement or mystical experience) is precisely what is not attended to in this kind of approach.

Jung defends his neglect by maintaining that psychology cannot deal with questions of artistic technique or evaluation.[22] This apology, which further justifies his concern with content and meaning, corresponds with the values of one of his early imaginal figures. We spoke of Philemon in Chapter One as Jung's preferred figure for imaginal engagements. Philemon was concerned with higher values of "meaning." Also present but less engaged was Ka, the craftsman, who was concerned not with meaning but with manifestation and beauty.

---

22. *CW*15, "Psychology and Literature," Intro., p. 85.

Jung employs deliberately the principle of compensation to explain the existence and function of visionary art. As noted earlier (Chapter Five) it is also a principle he uses to explain psychic life in general, as well as dreams. Dreams compensate and complement the situation of the psyche as a whole, by redressing its imbalances and filling out its phenomenology. This attitude toward the psyche regards it as a living entity in association with the more general patterns and movements of life itself.

An advantage of applying compensation to literary products is that it protects even the most unusual or unintelligible work from being simply dismissed. If a work is by definition a compensation in collective consciousness, even though it may appear absurd or nonsensical, it nonetheless has a meaning and function, if in no other way, then at least as a compensation. It was in fact this principle of compensation which shielded James Joyce's *Ulysses* from Jung's negativity in regard to it. Jung found the book empty, annoying and meaningless. It threatened his most cherished values in regard to higher spiritual meanings and ultimate significances. Though *Ulysses* was for Jung a "hellish monster-birth," boring, annoying and threatening in turn, he nonetheless had to admit some value to it. Precisely because it disturbed him it must be important, he reasoned, since one of the functions of great art is to disturb normal consciousness. Art introduces into awareness the inadmissible and compensates what in collective consciousness needs compensating. Jung achieves a rapprochement with *Ulysses* by viewing it as compensating for collective sentimentality. In this way he avoided the personal implications of his annoyance. But Jung's personal defense aside, the point remains that from a psychological perspective the unknown, the ununderstandable, the threatening has value. Because of the principle of compensation, it is just that which is most annoying. that cannot be dismissed out of hand.

Jung's principles in regard to literature are his principles in regard to dreams. Both are essentially creative products for which there are no immediate explanations.

> A great work of art is like a dream; for all its apparent obviousness it does not explain itself and is always ambiguous. A dream never say "you ought" or "this is the truth." It presents an image in much the same way as nature allows a plant grow, and it is up to us to draw conclusions.[23]

Jung's general attitude is regard to art, dream, and nature respects their basic ambiguity. They simply are, and do not issue unequivocally in human application. A dream is not concerned with whether one ought or ought not to do something. It will not say "this is the truth." As an image a dream simply represents itself, and it is up to the interpreter to draw what conclusions he may.

In this passage Jung places image as a primary rather than a derived or secondary phenomenon. Image represents nothing other than itself. It is not a disguised content, as Freud would have it, referring us to something more real or important. One may work with the image for implications, through interpretation, but these implications are like reverberations and never replace the image itself. In this view interpretation becomes a craft of working with, an activity secondary to the original image. This attitude of respect for the image is also reflected in Jung's definition of the symbol.

> [The symbol] is not something derived or secondary, it is not symptomatic of something else, it is a true symbol—that is, expression for something real but unknown.[24]

This definition of symbol leads to a mode of dream interpretation that Jung characterizes as "purposive," "constructive,"

---

23. *CW*15: 161.
24. *CW*15: 148.

"prospective," and "finalistic."[25] Symbols or images (for Jung the terms are interchangeable) point dream interpretation beyond causal reduction to past events toward a prospective value. This attitude toward interpretation, stipulates that the image open outward toward the less known, and also that the known be interpreted in terms of the unknown (rather than the unknown in terms of the known, as in a reductive interpretation).

This opening outward, however, can be taken in two senses, both canonically Jungian. The opening outward becomes prophetic interpretation in terms of future events and developments—developments that can be taken quite literally. But one may also follow Jung's more phenomenological, aesthetic attitude, in which developments need not be taken as linear or literal. From this point of view the opening-out prospectiveness of the image can be seen as a movement or potentiality, a fertility within the image itself, created by its particular tensions and patternings. The linear is, in other words, only one kind of movement; there are other kinds that may be recognized aesthetically. We might characterize this restless movement as a generativity or fertility in the image itself.

An imagistic interpretation would attempt to orient itself from some point in this generativity or fertility. The point determined as most generative, which interpretation would take as a bearing, depends to some extent on the perspective and preference of the interpreter. Before proceeding further we must address this question of perspective to see what Jung means by it and how he uses it.

---

25. Cf. Chapter Five, note 5.

Perspectivism

Early on Jung was aware of the role of subjectivity, or perspective, in regard to what was being seen. That an individual might have no assumptions Jung considered "impossible even if one exercises the most rigorous self-criticism, for one is oneself the biggest of all one's assumptions, and the one with the gravest consequences…as I am so will I proceed."[26] The way an individual regards exterior events takes on color inevitably from his assumptions and personal perspectives. When there is no possibility of seeing in a way entirely objective, the best one can do to be moderately objective is become aware of one's perspective.

> The demand that [an individual] should see *only* objectively is quite out of the question, for it is impossible. We must be satisfied if he does not see *too* subjectively.[27]

Even if observations are proved to accord with the "facts," these are not necessarily generalizable beyond the situation in which they are determined.

> That the subjective observation and interpretation accord with the objective facts proves the truth of the interpretation only in so far as the latter makes no pretence to be generally valid, but valid only for that area of the object which is being considered.[28]

For Jung it was not that the "object" or facts were not there to be seen, but, more positively, that the perspective adopted enabled the viewer to see things that could not be seen from other points of view. Thus the subjectivity of perspective and its inevitable projections are not necessarily to be avoided. They enable one to see things of psychological interest.

---

26. *CW*16: 543.
27. *CW*6: 10.
28. Ibid.

It is just the beam in one's own eye that enables one to detect the mote in one's brother's eye. The beam in one's own eye...does not prove that one's brother has no mote in his. But the impairment of one's own vision might easily give rise to a general theory that all motes are beams.[29]

For Jung the danger of perspective is not projection as such, but rather the tendency to generalize, i.e., to form a general theory on the basis of that projection.

Though Jung repeatedly notes the influence of perspective in observation, he is nonetheless in this matter essentially a scientist for whom the psyche is an entity to be observed and comprehended. In this vein he maintains that the job of the psychologist is to discover laws "which are merely abbreviated expressions for many diverse processes that are yet conceived to be somehow correlated."[30]

Jung treats perspective generally as one of several possible approaches to a given entity. Different sides of an object are revealed in accord with the perspective by which it is seen, but the object is not actually changed by the viewing. A single perspective cannot "embrace the whole, but must be content to shed light only on single parts of the total phenomenon."[31] Jung assumes that there is a fixed object to be seen and a truth to be known about it. Given enough perspectives, the object and its truth could presumably be grasped absolutely. The task is to recognize subjectivity in order to achieve a "scientific and impartial evaluation of a psyche different from that of the observing subject."[32] To recognize subjectivity is to be impartial, which is not to say without perspective.

----

29. Ibid.
30. *CW*6: 9.
31. *CW*15, p. 85.
32. *CW*6: 11.

Jung regards the viewpoint of psychology as such perspective. In "Psychology and Literature" he warns that

> the psychologist should constantly bear in mind that his hypothesis is no more at first than the expression of his own subjective premise and can therefore never lay claim to general validity.[33]

It is odd that Jung should qualify his statement to read "at first," implying that the psychologist's hypothesis is only initially subjective, as though later it might perhaps not be. In regard to literature Jung remains aware that his role is as a scientist. From this position he characterizes psychology as a discipline concerned with causality.

> Psychology and aesthetics will always have to turn to one another for help, and the one will not invalidate the other. It is an important principle of psychology that any given psychic material can be shown to derive from causal antecedents; it is a principle of aesthetics that a psychic product can be regarded as existing in and for itself.[34]

It is when Jung is in his scientific role that he is concerned with issues of perspective and subjectivity. He is concerned as a scientist seeking access to the facts of the psyche as an objective entity. In its relation to literature, Jung characterizes psychology as focusing on causality, but he actually proceeds otherwise in his written commentaries. Within these we seldom see him making causal connections—in fact he consciously forgoes this activity, characterizing lesser literature as not worth the effort and too obvious or "psychological" to be of interest. Greater (visionary) literature he also feels should not be subjected to merely causal thinking. His own approach, then, is to compare, amplify and construct general groupings (such as those of personal and visionary art).

---

33. *CW*15, p. 85.
34. *CW*15: 135.

The advantage of Jung's approach to literature is that he leaves it more or less intact. By not subjecting it to causal, psychological thinking and avoiding psychological reductions, he lets it be as subsistent phenomena. Perhaps his awareness of the limitations of psychological perspective aids him here, enabling him to put scientific causality aside.

What he seems less aware of is the limitation of the viewpoint by which he does approach literature. This viewpoint, as we saw with Joyce's *Ulysses* and in the case of Picasso's drawings, is concerned with meaningfulness and an overriding sense of symbolic, spiritual "wholeness." Jung views the plight of modern man as a search for meaning, and this meaning for him has to do with a balancing of perspectives between opposing opposites.

Wholeness and balance are in fact Jung's perspectival desiderata, and constitute the one perspective of which he is·unaware. What blinds him to it as a perspective is his underlying (scientific) assumption that events can indeed be known, given the proper combination of viewpoints. Jung's thinking in terms of perspectival balances goes somewhat as follows: if one's conscious perspective (the perspective to which one is habituated) has access to one side of the truth (which it has by definition), the other side of the truth will come through the opposite perspective. Unfortunately Jung goes on to specify these perspectives, listing them as introversion versus extraversion; thinking versus feeling; sensation versus intuition. So specified and described by Jung—as we will see when we get to types in the following section—the situation is now one of knowing not only what is known through the usual perspective (e.g., thinking-sensation) but also what is not known (e.g., feeling-intuition). To get to the truth of the matter, one need only combine these perspectives.

Though Jung has enough instinctual respect for phenomena (literary or psychological) that he never actually proceeds this

simplistically, his theory is an implicit justification of such pro-
cedures (as exemplified in much literary commentary of later
Jungians). A commitment to this kind of theory and procedure
obstructs imaginal approaches based on an *esse in anima*. Since
esse in anima implies, as we have argued, a relativization of oppositional categories, one can draw from it a more radical perspectivism, in which changes in one perspective effect changes in
others. The position from which one imagines an object affects
it and vice-versa, not because the object is a fact but because it
is part of an interrelation of viewer and viewed. Imagined from
within an *unus mundus*, perspective becomes interconnected
with what is viewed, and the concern becomes not one of sepa-
rating the two but of examining the manner and effect of their
interactions, of achieving *precise* descriptions rather than objective ones. The lack of generativity of which Jungian thought is
frequently accused has not, as is often presumed, to do with its
lack of scientific rigor and penchant for interior reflection and
mystical transcendence. The problem has to do with its attempts
to be comprehensive and systematic, to represent "wholeness."
The result is a spiritualized logocentrism. Jung's phenomenal
attitude, based on *esse in anima*, fails not because it is phenomenal or non-objective, but because he does not carry his phenomenology far enough to make it no longer a construction about
reality or even a perspective on it, but rather an imaginal position within reality.[35]

---

35. The reality to which we are here referring is what Creeley calls "actuality": "The real is what we value in real estate, and has to do with the things
of this life; res, re-possession, thing... But the actual has got that 'act' in it:
'actus, an ACT'...which is to say, the tree is real, but when you hit it, it's actual."
"The Creative," in Robert Creeley, *Sparrow* 6 (1973), n. pag.

Types

Related to the problem of perspectivism is the problem of types, since these are Jung's way of limiting and organizing perspective. Types return us to the case of the archeologist (Chapter Five). After his description and discussion, Jung remarks:

> The case I have just described is not unique, it is typical of a whole class, for which one of our poets has created a universally valid model. The poet is Spitteler, and the model is *Imago*. I take it that the course of *that* case is known.[36]

Typing is for Jung a way of universalizing. Things that recur over time may be grouped together, i.e., may be seen as having similar, not merely accidental, traits, which are then organized as types. Jung maintains that types are not pre-existent, *deductio a priori*, but empirically derived.[37] But the frequency with which he groups in terms of types and the tenacity with which he holds to them has more than an empirical flow.

Jung's tendency to think in types appears as early as 1904 in his association studies, in which he notes six types of association.[38] His most comprehensive statement is *Psychological Types* (1921). In this massive work he traces the history of some basic notions in Western thought by conceiving them in terms of attitude types and function types.

The difficulty with types, as with other categorizations, is that the unique individual is obscured for the sake of a more general prefiguring. Precise individuality is subsumed under fuzzy generalities. But types give a way of organizing and thus handling

---

36. *CW*6: 355. For a discussion of the significance of Spitteler's *Imago*, see Ellenberger, *The Discovery of the Unconscious*, 794–95.

37. *CW*6: 4.

38. *CW*2: 422–90.

a variety of different modes of thinking and being without con-
demning any. The difference between Tertullian and Origen,
Goethe and Schiller, or Freud and Adler is, according to Jung,
typological. It is not that one of these thinkers is right and the others wrong but that they each have a different purchase on reality. Thus types support perspectivism. But types also limit it. In
Jung's system there are only two possible attitudes and four functions (in various combinations, sixteen possibilities). The result is
a limited perspectivism, the purpose of which is to enable a more
objective viewing, one aware of its typological limitations.

Typological thinking implies a distrust of individual viewpoints, as if they are each in themselves inadequate and taken
together are a babel of unlimited multiplicity. This distrust goes
hand in glove with Jung's logocentric attitude. From the viewpoint of system, phenomena outside taxonomy appear disordered and chaotic. Just as he retreats from the immediacy of
the "image" into constructs composed of inner/outer, conscious/
unconscious distinctions, here, too, opening a way to perspectivism, he then attempts to control the notion by quantifying and
limiting it.

A theory of types can obviate more organic or inherent modes
of organizing. The psyche's own forms and the inherent order
of its activities—as maintained in Jung's theory of archetypes,
images, fantasy, and even in the autonomous personalities of
somnambulism—are here forgotten. Logocentrism encourages
this kind of forgetting, essentially Jung's forgetfulness of his aesthetic anima.

CHAPTER SEVEN

The Making of Interpretation

L et us return to Jung's aesthetic anima to reorient our perspective on some of the issues we have raised. We have seen that many of Jung's awarenesses contain the potentials for a psychology articulated from a basis in the imagination. Among these are Jung's notion of *esse in anima,* the primacy of the image, the formative potential of archetypes, the psyche's multiplicity, and the importance of the unknown, or unconscious. Jung never uses these grounds to articulate a psychopoetics fully because he is also concerned with and compromised by his scientific point of view, and its tendency to conceptual rather than imagistic thought.

One of Jung's objections to the aesthetic anima who tells him that he is doing art is that, contrary to her claim, he is doing not art but nature:

> This time I caught her and said, "No, it is not art! On the contrary, it is nature," and prepared myself for an argument. When nothing of the sort occurred, I reflected that the "woman within me" did not have the speech centers I had.[1]

Let us entertain the possibility that the anima fails to respond to Jung not because she has no speech centers but because she does not appreciate his distinction between art and nature. For her art and nature may not be dissimilar.

When Jung is in his scientific mode, nature appears to him a factual entity, *natura naturata*—something that exists which can

---

1. *MDR,* 186.

be explored and about which discoveries can be made. From an anima's, or aesthetic point of view, however, nature may appear less a matter of fact and more a matter of making or process, *natura naturans*. In this view "facts" may be used as handles, i.e., as operational terms, but facts are not simply data.

This attitude is consonant with the vision of Jacques Maritain, who concerned himself with the interrelation between the processes of art and the processes of nature. In his view human interiority, which he characterized as "subjective intuition," is known at the same moment and within the same experience as nature is known.

> Poetic intuition is filled with the subjectivity of the poet as well as with the thing grasped, since the thing grasped and the subjectivity are known together in the same obscure experience, and since the thing grasped is grasped only through its affective resonance in and union with the subjectivity.[2]

The artist's subjectivity is known together with its object, since its object is itself in the process of making. Thus the craftsman "tries to imitate secret workings and inner ways of the operation of nature."[3] This notion of art as imitating not nature as "the thing grasped" but nature's operations leads to a mimetic theory of art in which is emphasized the imitation of the action of nature rather than its object. According to Maritain, an "affective connaturality" is responsible for this mimesis:

> Poetic knowledge...is a specific kind of knowledge through inclination or connaturality—let us say a knowledge through affective connaturality which essentially relates to the creativity of the spirit and tends to express itself in a work.[4]

---

2. Maritain, *Creative Intuition in Art and Poetry*, 127.
3. Ibid., 129.
4. Ibid., 118.

Connaturality implies a making through correspondences with nature's own. The Islamic scholar Henry Corbin has this sense of correspondences in mind when he characterizes symbols as "symbolizing with" rather than "symbolic to" their referents.[5] The kind of making implied here proceeds by way of similarities, reverberations, and improvisations mimetic with, or paralleling natural movements and processes.

But nature is complex and exhibits different kinds of movements and processes. Thus to work mimetically through natural correspondences need not imply direct analogical correspondence or unidirectional movements. To characterize nature Jung quotes the alchemical maxim, "Nature rejoices in nature, nature subdues nature, and nature conquers nature."[6] This maxim, which attests to the complexity of "nature," mitigates a more simpleminded mimeticism.

We are concerned in this chapter with the art of interpretation. Following Maritain's view of nature as always in the process of making and the artist as engaging connaturally by correspondences with this process, let us extend this view to an image of the making of interpretation. Just as the dream is a making, not a disguise, so an interpretation is a making like the dream. All three function similarly; they are natural operations, or at least parallel. Dream, psychic process, and interpretation are all mimetic. From this perspective, interpretation may be regarded as a secondary activity performed by the interpreter upon the more primary level of making given in the dream.

---

5. Henry Corbin, *Avicenna and the Visionary Recital,* translated by Willard R. Trask (New York: Pantheon, 1960), 261; cf. also p. 31 and his "Mundus Imaginalis, or the Imaginary and the Imaginal," translated by Ruth Horine, *Spring: An Annual of Archetypal Psychology and Jungian Thought* (1972): 9.

6. *CW* 13: 426.

The advantage of this view for a psychopoetic hermeneutics is that it ties the interpretation closely to the dream, so that the dream is given value as a phenomenal manifestation, mimetic like the psyche itself. In this view, the dream is not simply a disguise for the psyche's workings, rather it corresponds with them. And the dream does not depend on interpretation for its meaning, but by manifesting it has already rendered its own kind of meaning.

Another corollary of this attitude of correspondences is that the evaluative judgments made in an interpretation correspond with evaluative processes in the dream itself. As an artistic object, the dream shows values which it has rendered in various ways, the shapes of which appear as the manifest shape of the dream. In an interpretation (if the interpretation is not merely a copy of the original tricked out with amplificatory parallels) this shape must be re-rendered but in a way fitting to or made possible by the original—within the same tone or key, yet as a contrasting variation or improvisation of it.

To avoid mixing too many metaphors at this point, let us return to Jung's own terms. Earlier we observed that Jung defines symbol as "something real but unknown" and that this definition led to a mode of interpretation he distinguished as purposive, prospective, constructive, or finalistic—characterizing the image as if it "opened outward" toward the less known.[7] This "opening outward" we called the point of fertility, or generativity, in the image to designate it as the place from which the new making begins. The new making of the interpretation commences, in other words, where the original image invites this possibility through an oddity or a conundrum that undoes or opens up the original image.

---

7. *CW* 15: 148.

To say that the interpretation works mimetically along with the dream's own processes is to say that it works through similarities of movement, possibilities given with the dream's tone and the nature of its particular imagery. The unusual or the unknown invites this secondary making, since it is at such points that the image opens outward. Interpretation is not mimetic in copying the dream as object, *naturata,* but it is mimetic in responding to, working with and off its processes. We shall return to these notions, with an example, after these few considerations.

Another matter of concern for a psychopoetics of interpretation has to do with the object upon which the interpreter works. In accord with Jung, let us consider this object the "image." Since image, by Jung's definition, is located in an imaginal realm between polarities, image is not an object in any literal sense, but it is nonetheless a clearly demarcated entity, thus an "object" in the metaphorical sense, an identity upon which one focuses *as though* it were separate from the interpreter's processes. This distinction between subject and object need not be considered a "subject-object split," but from a psychopoetic point of view may be regarded as a convention befitting an activity imagined as a crafting. The distinction is similar to one which Maritain makes concerning man and nature in which each keeps its identity though they interpenetrate each other.[8]

The importance of having an object to work on that is separate from the activity of interpretation is that its otherness requires the interpreter to be drawn out of himself, forced to work with an entity felt as foreign to himself. This otherness enables the interpreter to discover germinating forms and

---

8. "Each of the two terms involved [man and nature] remains what it is, it keeps its essential identity, it even asserts more powerfully this identity of its own, while it suffers the contagion or impregnation of the other" (Maritain, *Creative Intuition in Art and Poetry,* 5).

processes that lead beyond and thus change, his or her initial sense of boundaries. We have seen this otherness (cf. Chapter Three) as essential to depth psychology's underlying aesthetic. The unconscious, the not-known beyond-ego consciousness, requires of psychological work a continuous movement beyond self-established familiarities.

A sense of distance is also important to the imagination of craft, by which we mean a distance between the worker and that which is worked. The participation mystique that Jung spoke of ambivalently, both warning of its unconscious, noncritical quality and affirming it as a means by which he himself proceeded, is similar to the sense of mimesis we have described, provided it is accompanied by the element of craft. The dissolution of boundaries and mimetic enactment with other processes that characterize participation mystique are necessary but not sufficient for activities of psychopoetic making; another kind of distance must be operative. This impersonality, which Jung in his scientific stance mistakes for an objectivity, may be better characterized for our purposes as an attitude or stance of the craftsman toward his or her work. It is the attitude of which Maritain speaks as "disinterested" and that T.S. Eliot refers to when he speaks of poetry as a giving up of personality, not a scientific distancing or ego-identified detachment, but a distancing of the maker or craftsman from that which is crafted.[9] The attitude of craftsman requires a persona such that the personal ego, with its personal feelings and attitudes, is disengaged from the process. We saw this use of persona in Jung's case study of Helena Preiswerk, where it gave to the proceedings a fictional texture from which Jung the individual could effect a distancing. Though in

9. Ibid., 143; "Tradition and the Individual Talent," in T.S. Eliot, *The Sacred Wood: Essays on Poetry and Criticism* (London: Methuen, 1960), 47–59.

this case the persona was scientific and Jung was unaware of it as a persona, its effect for us is a fictional distancing.

The image on which the interpreter works, though an entity with borders and boundaries of identity, need not be singular or even visual. Jung regards language, for example, as an image.[10] The image may be a particular entity in a dream or a configuration in the dream, the dream in its entirety, the dream within a situation, symptom, the course of an illness, etc. The image is simply that upon which the work of crafting focuses as "given and non-negotiable."[11] In this way a tension is maintained between the worker and the non-malleability or resistance of that which is worked.

This resistance is necessary for the tension of psychological making. We have seen the frequency and the· determination with which Jung used categorical oppositions, contrasts, and divisions in the construction of all of his major concepts. We have noted the liability of these oppositions for a work based on image. Nonetheless, if we regard them as themselves images— the ones necessary to Jung's constructions—we can inquire as to their effect in the psychopoiesis of his system. Certainly one effect has been to create tension.

Tension, we have argued, is a basic requirement for an aesthetics in depth psychology. The unknown, the unconscious, is a primary and necessary structural component and a necessary *dunamis* for the movement of psychical processes, and its value should be reflected in the activity of interpretation. As a negation, the unconscious creates tension; in working with an image, tension guides the directional movement of the interpretation.

---

10. *CW* 9.1: 271.

11. "Poetry: A Note in Ontology," in John Crowe Ransom, *The World's Body* (Baton Rouge: Louisiana State University Press, 1938), 118.

This sense of direction in a dream and its interpretation orients the processes of elaboration.

To proceed by way of tensions implies a poiesis that works through an unbalancing of what has been established. Though this process may seem opposed to Jung in his systematic mode (in his emphasis on balance and wholeness, and consequent use of compensation as an interpretive principle), it is closer to what in fact he does. When he looks at dreams from the finalist perspective he necessarily upsets the structures by which the dream has been established. By saying the dream points toward something beyond itself, he unhinges and unbalances the dream image, since it is now on the way toward something other, which other is the making of interpretation.

This unbalancing in order to make may be seen as an effect of Jung's aesthetic anima. Earlier we saw her unbalance his mandalic structures, and all through these chapters we have seen her as opposed to his systematic constructions. In her penchant for making, and in the unique, the particularity of sensuous manifestations, the anima serves in Jung's work to break established systems. Whether she challenges the structures he proposes in theory but does not act on in practice, or the contradictions between his theories, or the variety of his interpretive actions, Jung's anima breaks what is established and in so doing creates movement and direction. To follow this anima movement in a dream we must orient our interpretation in terms of oddities and unbalances specific to the image with which we are working.

To apply this sense of making more concretely to what has been said, let us return to the delusional archeologist. The fantasy of this patient, which Jung reported in detail, involved battles and a movement from chaos to a feeling of being "exalted and strengthened by a strange, soothing feeling that someone was watching his struggles—that his loved one saw all of this from afar." Jung notes that this was the period during which the patient was physically violent toward his attendants. After this point there proceeded more fantasies, battles, and a final victory. Then, as the patient drew near his loved one, his illness ceased and he awoke as from a long dream.

Let us consider as the object of our focus the fantasy as a whole. In general the images it uses are fairly trite. The action is repetitive, the language grandiose—there is one battle after another—and the particular images, though they announce emotion are, at least in Jung's report, quite typical. There is "a sea of blood and fire," "everywhere conflagrations," "volcanic outbursts," earthquakes," "tremendous battles in which nation was hurled on nation." The dreamer was "in the midst of...fighters, wrestling, defending himself, enduring unutterable misery and pain."[12] Despite the lurid nature of the fantasy, it is basically conventional in that nothing is outre. There is emotion, but no imaginal tension.

The images of this fantasy are archetypal—i.e., often instanced in myth, art, literature and religion. But paralleling or amplifying is of no particular interpretive interest, since the images appear in a manner so unoriginating and conventional. Yet sometimes archetypal images are of great interest, though never because they are archetypal. Place and function within the overall context is crucial for determining their value since, as we have argued, the making of interpretation takes its orientation from the odd or unknown within the original image.

Jung's observation that the battling activities in the patient's fantasy corresponded with his physical violence toward his attendants is also of little help in orienting interpretation, though instructive on a therapeutic level as a means of patient

---

12. *CW* 3: 352.

management. This correspondence explains his behavior, but explanation is not interpretation. An explanation does not lead beyond the explained, but tends further to establish it. At its worst, when explanation is accompanied by a one-directional sense of causality (the patient was violent *because* he was having violent fantasies), the reasons for what is already known (his violence) are fixed so that there is little possibility for other sorts of interpretive movement.

The coincidence of violence and fantasy that Jung unknowingly identifies cannot serve 'for him as a causal explanation. It does disclose a parallel between two phenomena and draws further attention to them. When comparison is used in this way, there is no claim that one thing (either fantasy or behavior) causes the other.

Psychopoetically a thickening occurs as a result of this likening. Comparisons have the advantage of implying interconnections (correspondences) without the one-directional limitation of causality. By comparing and paralleling events, Jung places notions of causality in a mid-realm, in this case between behavior and fantasy, so that neither behavior nor fantasy can be reduced to one another. This in-between realm, which we elaborated as the realm of anima, *esse in anima,* is once again a central focus for the technique of psychological making, but it is a focus which may easily be obscured.

One way this loss of focus can occur is through an overelaborate use of parallels and amplifications in which the original object of concern gets lost, along with the space of anima. Anima as a mid-realm makes sense only insofar as it is genuinely fruitful for imagination. It is not that the anima is literally fixed at a place between two points but that, when a situation is constructed oppositionally, the most fertile place for imagination is in between. In the technique of amplification however, anima becomes a limit, or a tactful boundary to keep comparisons from straying too far from the original. Ideally it fills it out, sounds it larger, rather than detracts from it. Measure here holds the tension by allowing parallels to unfold, enlarging the scope and increasing reverberation at no expense to the original figure.

If interpretation is meant to value the unknown, it may best find its orientation from a place in the image that shows some oddity or surprise. In Jung's patient's fantasy, after the standard battle scenes, the next image is the "feeling of being watched from afar." This image is of some interest in that it is at least more particular.

Not all battles are watched from afar. Also the focus shifts from an engagement in the battle to its being watched. In this shift a space is created between the heroic struggle and that for which the struggle was undertaken.

The fantasy continues. There are more battles: "He felt his strength increasing and saw himself at the head of great armies which he would lead to victory. Then more battles, and victory at last." One might expect the theme of victory to be important since it is archetypal, and it culminates and resolves the action. But the image does not rest with this standard resolution. According to the text, the fantasy ends with the moment of drawing near. "As he drew near her the illness ceased, and he awoke from a long dream." This odd detail of drawing near creates a slight disjunction from the cliche of final union and consummation. By means of this difference a tension and irony is preserved; interpretive interest is awakened, as though until then it, too, had been asleep. This moment, which is of interest in its difference, tension, and irony, is the point of most value for interpretation, since it is here that the typicality of the fantasy shows some variation, allowing an opening into an area less known and thus into a possibility for making.

Orienting the interpretation at this point places it in a mid-realm of awareness, so that drawing near is important, yet not wholly, not literally so. The image is a fantasy and if, as Jung says, "fantasy creates reality," then what we are dealing with is an aesthetic sense of feeling prior to and more important than that of drawing into physical proximity with the actual woman. For this interpretive sense to be effectively conjured up, the interpretation must begin at the proper place, at the point of most value.

Should the interpretation have other aims than those we have termed aesthetic, it will choose other aspects of the fantasy to emphasize. If the goal of the interpretation is reality adaptation, and reality is considered the "fact" that this patient will never actually unite with the woman of his dreams, then the fantasy will be read as a compensatory wish-fulfillment. If the goal is wholeness of personality, then the fantasy will be seen as an attempt to "integrate" the feminine. If it is ego development, then the fantasy of battles and victory will become the means of acquiring strength and of putting enemies to flight.

These interpretations, though they draw upon aspects of the fantasy, differ from the approach we have offered in that they do not take their orientation from the text but from ideas and values outside the text—ideas such as "reality adaptation," wholeness of personality and ego development. In orienting, as we have, from within the text, values such as movement, tension, irony, particularity, and atypicality guide our approach.

Though there are of course other aesthetic values that, given the proper circumstances, might have played a role—e.g., unity, balance, beauty—in this particular text anima as longing is emphasized so that her movement (animation) and process become important. Even if the movement generated by longing were not overdetermined in this particular image, we have maintained anima as movement to be of essential psychological value. The value of the unconscious, the unknown, and Jung's purposive emphasis on that which is beyond the given—the anima's tendency to break stasis through a disbalancing for the sake of further making--all attest to a dynamic psychology based on movement. And there are many sorts of psychological movement—movements of deepening through stasis, of filling out, of gathering complexity, metamorphosing, changes in kind from one thing to another.

Interpretation raises a difficulty regarding its evaluation. What makes one interpretation better than another? By what criteria are they judged? We have offered one based on a of making, which assumes interpretation to be a mimetic activity like the psyche's creative processes, and noted guidelines for these processes having to do with tension, the unknown and the atypical. But ultimately the value of an interpretation depends for its effectiveness on the particular criteria invoked.

These criteria are relative to the context of the making, i.e., the kind of image being worked with, and the goals of the making. Because of this relativity an interpretation may work in one way and not in another, in a number of ways or in one very particular way. It may work to increase complexity, or tension, or a deeper level of reverberation. Or it may work to simplify direction and thus open possibilities.

Underlying these criteria is the release of anima that a good interpretation fosters. Movement may follow a path from the general to the precise, from the conceptual to the imagistic, from the abstract to the sensual—yet such paths are not prescribed. Otherwise they too would become programmatic, and anima and its motion stifled. Anima precludes programmatics. But in its movement (*kinesis*) it will open, close, raise, or deepen what is there into a condition not previously apparent in the given. Interpretive animation will affect the form of the interpreted material, by transforming, deforming or informing the given into a hitherto unknown shape. Further it will operate upon the fixities, literalisms, densities and naturalisms of the given so that more imaginal possibilities may proceed.

The interpretation offered above for the fantasy of Jung's patient worked toward opening beyond the known to awarenesses of a more imaginal quality. Since the value assumed by the interpretation forms also the criteria by which it is judged, an interpretation depends finally on itself. Whether an interpretation is ultimately true in an ontological sense or "right" in a moral sense is less important than its value for the activity of making.

Because of this binding interrelation between making and its values, the evaluation of interpretation is similar to the evaluation of any other psychological making, and the criteria like that of all psychopoiesis.

CHAPTER EIGHT

Psychopathology

Having shifted our position to a pragmatic approach based on *esse in anima,* we turn now to the question of psychopathology. As a practical art, depth psychology is concerned not only with the description or understanding of psychic events but more pointedly with the treatment and cure of the psyche's disorders. Thus psychological interpretation is generally oriented in terms of its implications for the treatment of pathology. But what is pathology?

There are those who hold that psychopathology is essentially a construction of the medical mind. By categorizing behaviors as pathological, the field of medicine reaffirms its normative values and standards, and thus its position of power. This criticism, for which Thomas Szasz is the outstanding spokesman, puts into question the means by which diagnostic judgments are made.[1]

Jung considered psychopathology to be normative and contextual to the extent that a behavior considered merely odd in one society or context might in another be labeled pathological.[2] In this sense diagnostic judgment is relative to the situation, historical period, and social climate in which the judgment is made. Though these factors influence diagnosis, they do not deny the existence of pathology.

---

1. Thomas Szasz, *The Ethics of Psychoanalysis; The Theory and Method of Autonomous Psychotherapy* (Syracuse, N.Y.: Syracuse University Press, 1988 [1965]).
2. *CW* 18: 72.

According to the medical historian Erwin Ackerknecht, mental disease is not only relative to the society, but some forms of mental illness in primitive societies are impossible even to conceptualize in our diagnostic terms.[3] Nevertheless the fact remains that all societies have behaviors they consider abnormal or pathological, and these are usually determined according to an individual's relative capability for a "minimum of adaptation and social functioning within his society."[4]

Though the criterion of abnormality and the evaluative schemes by which it is determined may appear different in different societies, their existence is constant and perhaps universal. Generally this behavior is distinguished from behavior that is merely strange or unusual—such as occurs through inspirational, mystical, shamanistic or drug-oriented states.

Our tradition of psychopathological description derives from a history of evaluative lore. A pioneering work in this regard was Emil Kraepelin's *Lehrbuch der Psychiatrie,* published in 1883.[5] In this work Kraepelin laid out a rational nosology and classification of mental illness, which included the introduction of "dementia praecox" and "manic-depressive illness" to the taxonomic scheme. Kraepelin's system was praised for the clarity it brought to the field of mental illness and was accepted for a time as the authoritative system for classificatory understanding.[6]

Since that time, further differentiations, qualifications and reorganizations have occurred. Schizophrenia replaced dementia praecox as a diagnostic term.[7] Disorders such as melancholia,

---

3. Erwin H. Ackerknecht, *A Short History of Psychiatry,* translated by Sulammith Wolff (New York and London: Hafner Publications, 1959), 6.

4. Ibid., 3.

5. *Lehrbuch der Psychiatrie,* 8th ed., 4 vols. (Leipzig: n. pub., 1909–15).

6. Ellenberger, *The Discovery of the Unconscious,* 285.

7. Eugen Bleuler, *Dementia Praecox or the Group of Schizophrenias,* translated by Joseph Zinkin (New York: International Universities Press, 1950).

classical hysterical, moral insanity have disappeared to reappear under different titles, or as qualification within larger categories. New syndromes such as "borderline personality," "narcissistic personality," bulimia, anorexia nervosa, have emerged. But despite these shifts in psychiatric conceptualization and nomenclature, pathological processes remain generally recognizable as pathological.

To contend that pathology is recognizable by those whose business is to recognize it is not to deny the variety of models used in explaining its mechanisms and theorizing about its psychodynamics. Jung himself conceives of psychopathology in several different ways. One of the models frequently informing his vision is that of an imbalance or one-sidedness of psychic functioning.

The psyche is always to some extent imbalanced in that conscious attention requires selection and emphasis for its directionality. But this imbalance, according to Jung, increases radically during phases of transition and in states generally characterized as neurotic.[8] To compensate the imbalance of this one-sided consciousness, the unconscious reappears in the form of symptoms, which disturb consciousness. Jung characterizes these compensatory mechanisms variously in terms of attitudinal orientations, functions of consciousness, the workings of "shadow," "anima," or "animus," or sometimes more generally as the unconscious itself.

This model imagines the psyche in terms of its tendency to seek equilibrium, but it also recognizes the psyche as alive and intentional. Aspects left out of consciousness are seen, when the situation is so constellated, as seeking recognition and inclusion, if not in one form then another, i.e., as a symptom.

---

8. *CW* 18: 667.

In recognizing this purposive quality of the symptom, Jung characterizes it as an attempt at self-cure.[9] Neurosis is in this sense fortunate, since it attempts to redress the psyche's imbalance by calling attention to itself symptomatically. The suffering of neurosis keeps the psyche from settling comfortably into habitual conscious attitudes.

But neurosis is also for Jung an inauthentic suffering (*uneigentliches Leiden*), in that it is essentially a suffering not of the underlying psychic conflict but of the neurosis.[10]

> Repression...causes an indirect suffering from something unreal, namely a neurosis. Neurotic suffering is an unconscious fraud and has no moral merit, as has real suffering.[11]

For Jung suffering is not necessarily pathological or to be avoided. He speaks of it as the "normal counterpole to happiness."[12] But neurotic suffering is indirect and fraudulent, what Freud calls a "compromise formation."[13] By partially expressing the repressed through the disguise of a symptom, neurosis enables repression to continue in a somewhat different form. Neurosis is in this way basically conservative and defensive.

Jung also draws on an energetic model for his explanations of psychopathology. This view, presented most thoroughly and lucidly in his essay "On Psychic Energy," regards neurosis in terms of its potentially transformative processes.[14] According to this model, when an individual is confronted with a difficulty, either externally or internally, for which his usual modes

---

9. *CW* 18: 1480, 386, 389.
10. *CW* 18: 383.
11. *CW* 17: 154.
12. *CW* 16: 179.
13. "The Defence Neuro-Psychoses," in Freud, *Collected Papers,* 1:163; "Hysterical Phantasies and Bisexuality," 2:56.
14. *CW* 8, pp. 3–66.

of adaptation are insufficient, progression of libido ceases and its regression occurs. In this regression opposites once conjoined now separate, and the individual finds himself without his usual ability to adapt. This failure of adaptation, typical of neurosis, forces the individual to come to terms with the "inner world" of his psyche.[15] If this situation is to be healed, according to Jung, a symbol must be produced by the unconscious. This symbol unites opposites in a new way and transforms psychic libido. Neurosis is cured through an "upgrading" of libido, i.e., through qualitative changes. Since this qualitative transformation of energy is the dynamic means by which the psyche works in general, neurosis becomes, when viewed through this model, a necessary occurrence. Conscious adaptation must fail in order that the psyche be transformed.

For our purposes the most interesting model Jung uses in his discussions of psychopathology, the most fruitful model in its implications for a psychopoiesis, is that which involves his theory of complexes. Complexes are the basic units by which the psyche is organized. According to Jung, "practically every [mental] association belongs to some complex or other."[16] Jung sometimes speaks of complexes as not only normal but desirable, as when he hazards that "the whole aim of education is to implant lasting complexes."[17]

The complex is defined as feeling-toned groups of associations in the unconscious.[18] These associational structures based on affect are prior to intellection and necessary to its vitality.

---

15. *CW* 8: 6.

16. *CW* 8: 82.

17. *CW* 3: 90.

18. *CW* 2: 733. For Jung it was not dreams (as Freud maintained) but complexes that were "the *via regia* to the unconscious" (*CW* 8: 210).

Without this feeling-tone "the idea is an empty shadow."[19] Feel-ing-tone is also formative for character, inclinations and drives.

> What is "primarily characterological" is, in the wider sense, the feeling-tone, whether it be too little or too much or per-verse; in the narrower sense it is the inclinations and drives, the basic psychological phenomena which make up man's empirical character.[20]

Jung speaks of the feeling-tone of the complex as similar to a musical motif.

> The leitmotiv, as a sort of feeling-tone, denotes a complex of ideas which is essential to the dramatic structure. Each time one or the other complex is stimulated by something some-one does or says, the relevant leitmotiv is sounded in one of its variations. It is exactly the same in ordinary psychic life: the leitmotivs are the feeling-tones of our complexes, our actions and moods are modulations of the leitmotivs.[21]

Complexes are therefore tied through melody and mood simi-larities, but these moods are multiple, since there are many com-plexes and many possible feeling-tones. This view of the psyche sees it as rich in its ability to combine and recombine in new constellations around energetic feeling motifs, which are at once its sources of motivation.

The advantage this has over Jung's structural model of bal-ances and energetic model of transformations is that the model based on complexes does not require generalized qualities as balanced contraries or characterized forces. Further, its muta-ble clusters avoid the one-dimensionality of linear imagining in terms of progression and regression. Complexes imply fields of association in which inner and outer, behavior and mood, co-exist and interconnect in potentially formative ways.

------

19. *CW*1: 221.
20. *CW*1: 220.
21. *CW*3: 80n.4.

The complex is thus the basis for both the creativity of genius and for pathology. "All new ideas and combinations of ideas are premeditated by the unconscious" complex.[22] In "Cryptomnesia" (1905)—to which we shall return later in this chapter—Jung compares hysteria with genius, maintaining that the psychological source for both is the same, and that within this complex source there are certain dangers:

> What kind of people seek these new combinations? They are the men of thought, who have finely differentiated brains coupled with the sensitivity of a woman and the emotionality of a child. They are the slenderest, most delicate branches on the great tree of humanity: they bear the flower and the fruit. Many become brittle too soon, many break off. Differentiation creates in its progress the fit as well as the unfit; wits are mingled with nitwits—there are too with genius and geniuses with follies.[23]

Then again:

> On this treacherous ground wander all who seek· new combinations of ideas. Woe to them if they do not continually exercise the most rigorous self-criticism![24]

It is not the source that differentiates the creative from the pathological individual. Both walk the same "treacherous ground" of originary complexes. What distinguishes the two has wholly to do with the manner (*die Art und Weise*) in which the complex is worked through (*verarbeitet*).[25] The artist works the ground directly from the image complex, and he does so with a "powerful means of expression" and directness of intention, whereas the neurotic is without directing ideas and possesses only feeble means.[26]

---

22. *CW*1: 172.
23. *CW*1: 175.
24. *CW*1: 175.
25. *CW*6: 970
26. *CW*3: 298f.

Jung differentiates often in his discussions of pathology between the complex as a potentially poetic substrate and the various forms of its pathological manifestation. In pathology, however, the complex, rather than being worked with directly, is avoided through various defensive counter-reactions.[27]

In his association studies Jung notes the reactions to complexes, what he calls "complex indicators," as sudden, erratic irruptions, disconnected whims, mannered combinations, stereotypical or superficial reactions, repetition, perseveration, verbigeration, blocking, amnesia, and egocentric reactions.[28] Whereas the complex itself may be seen to function analogically, by means of metonymy and condensation, double meanings, and irony, in pathology these qualities lose their presentational clarity and become through avoidance "sentiments d'incomplétude."[29] We must now examine pathological mechanisms in more detail.

One of the qualities characterizing pathology appears as egocentricity. The complex interrupts the ego's "peaceful cycle of egocentric ideas," so that the ego loses its "attention-tone" to the more powerfully affective constellation of the complex.[30] In a neurotic situation the ego attempts to regain this lost affect by constantly calling attention to itself. In the association experiment these egocentric responses show as associative references to the subject (responses such as "me," "mine," "I," or the use of one's own name). More generally in psychopathology this egocentricity is seen in the tendency to neologisms or made-up words. It is easier, and more in keeping with egocentric boundaries, narcissistically to invent a word than to search for an apt one in the common vocabulary.

---

27. *CW*3: 141.
28. *CW*3: 9-10, 1, 12, 16.
29. *CW*3: 218, 217, 222, 285, 313, 174.
30. *CW*3: 84.

Jung also views wish-fulfillment as essentially egocentric.[31] Through wish-fulfillment the psyche attempts to compensate or substitute for what seems personally lacking. Jung considers this person l wish-fulfillment not as how the psyche works in general (Freud's view) but how it works insofar as it is neurotic. In this view personalizing is seen as a mark of inadequate psychological making, as though when adequate the psyche's concerns are more than simply personal.

If the psyche is based on imaginative makings, its disorders are also disorders of the imagination. Thus diagnostic or psychiatric description may be seen as criticisms of the imagination, and, vice-versa, the imagination may be criticized for diagnostic content. For this reason it is not surprising that we find Jung, as in the following example, evaluating a patient's literary compositions in the process of arriving at a diagnosis:

> His compositions were closely written, looked clean and neat, and except for the copious use of foreign words the spelling was correct. They revealed an erudition of sorts, a very good memory...with great pressure of speech and forceful expressions. Prose pieces in literary style or in dialect were jumbled together with quotations from Schiller, verses...sentences in French, always with a connecting thread of meaning which, however, did not go very deep. No uniform, comprehensive idea could be found in any of his writings, except for an intense subjective feeling of his own value and an unbounded self-esteem. The language he used was sometimes full of deep pathos, sometimes deliberately paradoxical. He was ready to discuss his ideas, did not cling to them obstinately, but dropped them in order to turn to new problems.[32]

This description of Jung's reads a bit like a teacher criticizing a freshman theme. Indeed, Jung concludes:

---

31. *CW* 3: 299.
32. *CW* 1: 216.

This case reminds one forcibly of those miserable lives lived by poets and artists who, with small talent and indestructible optimism, eke out a hungry existence despite the fact that they possess quite enough intelligence to realize their social inadequacy in this form, and enough talent and energy, if applied in other directions, to do good an even outstanding work in an ordinary profession.[33]

Jung sees this case as having psychopathic features. Basically it is a mood disorder with "an excessively sanguine temperament, which serves as too mercurial a base for the intellectual process and...necessary continuity of feeling-tone."[34]

This disorder is also responsible for the patient's inability to recognize his lack of talent. Both his judgment and his talent are too mercurially based for either to go very deep. There is little self-awareness, since his "unbounded self-esteem" clouds the issue, making him unaware of the need for a "comprehensive idea" in either his work or his behavior.

Since the above case is a mood disorder, the behavior through which affect is enacted is central to the diagnosis. But also important for the differentiation of the diagnosis is the mode of his associations, the way his mind organizes as seen in his written work. From his behavior alone Jung might have diagnosed his disorder as organic, hysterical or even schizophrenic, with mood swings as a secondary characteristic. The precise manner of the associations, the way in which the complex is worked, is essential in the differentiation of the diagnosis.

Also important in he diagnosis of pathology are various degrees of irrelevancy, the tendency to "talk around" the complex, as though to obscure it or fill it up with excess verbiage (verbigeration).[35] And the use of what Jung calls "power words" is

---

33. *CW*1: 219.
34. *CW*1: 220.
35. *CW*31 179.

diagnostically significant. As the term implies, these are words which pretend to more emphasis or importance than appears justified by the context. According to Jung, power words are attempts to accentuate "the value of the personality" by exorcising possibilities of doubt.[36]

Monotony, stereotypy, repetition of style and/or content are also important in psychological diagnosis. At their most extreme they point to disorders of a schizophrenic nature, in which case they are accompanied by deprivation of thought and a separation of thought and affect (blunted affect).[37] In associations these stereotypies sometimes show as collective or unoriginal responses. Clanging rhymes, current jingles or popular maxims show up as "well-worn combinations of phrase or sound," according to Jung, when a person is uncertain of his perhaps more original or individual responses.[38] Superficiality is of as much relevance diagnostically as are more obviously pathological features, such as dissociation.

Dissociation appears as sudden disjunction, eruptions in the associative field. What characterizes them as dissociations (rather than evidence of originality) is the sense that they are substituting for something else—i.e., compensating some level of the psyche rather than expressing it. As a result they may appear banal and uninteresting, sometimes sentimental, sometimes without sentiment at all.[39] But in any case, there is something personal or egocentric implied by the palpable cover-up of the original image. Pathology is thus characterized as defensive, more superficial, less genuine than what is sensed as the underlying image complex.

---

36. *CW* 3: 155.
37. *CW* 3: 217.
38. *CW* 3: 135.
39. *CW* 18: 627; *CW* 3: 507–8.

These diagnostic judgments of Jung's (which are typical of psychiatric judgment in general) rest willy-nilly on aesthetic assumptions. Evaluations are made regarding the quality of genuineness or authenticity in patterns of associative processes. These processes appear in feeling, intellection, and behavior as manifestations of complex substrates. So far we have regarded pathology as a mis-making with these complexes. In this way pathology has been put in a relation between the original manifestation and the psyche's way of working with it such that the pathological and the creative are perceived as quite distinct. Though this distinction between the pathological and the creative is Jung's normal attitude, he sometimes speaks of them as mutually implicated.

In his essay "Cryptomnesia" Jung was concerned with tracing the roots of creativity in hysteria. He viewed cryptomnesia, or plagiarizing, as the result of a hysterical tendency to dissolve personal boundaries and merge with, and thus unconsciously borrow from, others. Jung wrote this essay, which first appeared in the weekly *Die Zukunft*, in defense of the drama critic Siegfried Jacobsohn who, accused of plagiarizing, claimed he was unaware of having done so.[40] Whereas this denial precipitated conjectures from the medical community regarding possible disorders of an organic sort (that he was the victim of a brain lesion, and did not know what he was doing), Jung came to his defense with a psychological argument regarding the similarity between creative and hysterical borrowing.

In this article Jung speaks of originality as the ability to create new combinations from already existent material. Since creativity has to do with this ability to combine, rather than with the material itself, it depends to a large extent on "indirect" memories

---

40. "Kryptomnesie," *Die Zukunft* 13 (1905); trans. in *CW* 1, pp. 95-108.

and unconscious associations. The unconscious, which Jung here defines broadly as "everything that is not represented in consciousness, whether momentarily or permanently," contains an immense number of memory associations or complexes.[41] Only some of these are recognized as memories. Others, insofar as they have been creatively reorganized, are experienced as fortuitous, "chance ideas" (*Einfall*), and groundless, since they have been detached from their original contexts.

Hysteria may be considered as exaggeration or caricature of this detachment. Typically in hysteria reactions appear unfitting, and without associative linkages to the situations in which they are enacted. Insofar as both the artist and the hysteric work from this realm of autonomous complexes, the connections and sources of which are unknown, they share certain difficulties. One is the all too human desire to employ this realm to satisfy private wishes and hopes.

> Since, in the airy world of thought, one usually finds what one seeks, and gets what one wishes, the man who seeks new ideas will also be the most easily enchanted with the deceptive gifts of the psyche...What poet or composer has not been so beguiled by certain of his ideas as to believe in their novelty? We believe what we wish to believe. Even the greatest and most original genius is not free from human wishes and their all-too-human consequences.[42]

Apparently, the wish for novelty leads to forgetting. Jung seems to be talking about more here than the anxiety of influence; he speaks of the realm of complexes which, shared by the artist and the hysteric, attest to the proximity of genius and pathology.

Hysteria in this context is less a defense against the complex, as usually regarded, than a too immediate, personal, or

---

41. *CW*1: 166n.2.
42. *CW*1: 174.

unworked reaction—one which shows a "lack of self-control and self-criticism." Since genius, too, requires a certain loss of consciousness and lack of self-control to allow the formation of new combinations, the states of genius and hysteria do indeed have something in common. Jung is explicit about the connection:

> We can assert with confidence that unless the hysterical mentality is present to a greater or lesser degree genius is not possible. As Schopenhauer rightly says, the characteristic of the genius is great sensibility, something of the mimosa-like quality of the hysteric. Geniuses also have other qualities in common with hysterical persons.[43]

Jung goes on to suggest that the genius, like the hysteric, must deal with "an outsized psychic complex." To the extent that he is able to do this, he succeeds; to the extent that he fails, he exhibits symptoms.[44]

The role of consciousness in this process is that of servant or "slave."[45] Consciousness does not lead but serves the work by sorting through complexes and shaping them into coherent and effective forms. These larger forms consist essentially of old material. Even the masters borrow from what has gone before.

> Only the combinations are new, not the material, which hardly alters at all, or only very slowly and almost imperceptibly. Have we not seen all Böcklin's hues already in the old masters? And were not the fingers, arms, legs, noses, and throats of Michelangelo's statues all somehow prefigured in antiquity? The smallest parts of a master work are certainly always old, even the next largest, the combined units, are mostly taken over from somewhere else; and in the last resort a master will not scorn to incorporate whole chunks of the past in a new work. Our psyche is not so fabulously rich that it can build from scratch each time. Neither does

---

43. *CW*1: 175.
44. *CW*1: 176.
45. *CW*1: 177.

nature. One can see from our prisons, hospitals, and lunatic asylums at what enormous cost nature takes a little step forward; she builds laboriously on what has gone before.[46] Jung's view of "nature" here reveals a sober distrust of progress and of creative originality. For him creativity does not take wings but advances like coral on foregoing generations. For every movement forward a shadow is cast back, for every construction there is destruction, for every making a mis-making. Prisons, hospitals, lunatic asylums—housing nature's mishaps—accompany her developments. So, too, originality, creativity, and genius are closely allied with pathology. Both states—one applauded, the other eschewed—derive from the same unconscious ground of complexes.

In keeping with this troubled vision Jung's essay on cryptomnesia not surprisingly concludes that unconscious plagiarism, similar to that of the hysteric, occurs in works of genius as well. The example he offers in support repeats one he had offered earlier in "On the Psychology and Pathology of So-called Occult Phenomena."[47] The situation involves Nietzsche's *Thus Spake Zarathustra*, which contains details remarkably similar to those in a story published earlier by Justinus Kerner in his *Blätter aus Prevorst*. Since these details are peripheral in Nietzsche's work, Jung concludes they are merely traces picked up by Nietzsche and unconsciously stored since the time in his youth when he read Kerner's story. In the "abnormal mental state" in which Nietzsche, by his own account, wrote *Zarathustra*, the unconscious complex with which these memory traces were associated got constellated.

Thus cryptomnesia seems to Jung a possibility whenever deeper levels of the psyche are activated, as they inevitably are in

46. *CW* 1: 178.
47. *CW* 1: 140f.

creativity and in psychopathology. Both states draw on the same level of unconscious, autonomous complexes. The difference between the productions of a hysteric and those of a genius is that in the genius those fragments are built into new and meaningful structures. In both, however, the psychic process is "an automatic creative force.[48] The pathological and creative are not different in kind—the difference is in how they are crafted.

But in a sense pathology, too, is a making. When Jung emphasizes the banality, poor sentiment and non-originality of pathological productions, he is describing pathology from a vantage point from which he intuits more interesting possibilities.[49] This kind of intuition is essential to the clinician, feeding his creative desire from a remaking and upgrading of the original material.

The basic making that is pathology has its own kind of originality. Pathology departs from the usual; habits of thought, perception and feeling break down to reorganize along symptomatic lines. The originary force, the intensity with which the usual is broken, and the persuasiveness of the patterns that replace it, attest a creative power.

Indeed, psychopathology has been of utter importance for the field of depth psychology. Its originations have required that psychology shift its point of view to take into account what would otherwise appear incomprehensible. The role of psychopathology in Jung's work, as we have seen, has been a constant stimulus and challenge—in response to which his psychology developed into the shape we know.

We have traced this formational process beginning with Jung's breakdown, and have seen how his responses to it created the experiential basis for his later ideas. We explored the importance

---

48. *CW*1: 185.
49. *CW*3: 507; *CW*18: 627.

of his relation with his mediumistic cousin, Helene Preiswerk, and his fascination with her hysterical raptures and autonomous "personalities." We saw how his observations of the woman with the pince-nez and feathers gave him a narrative tactic with which he could counter medical materialism by insisting on the importance of a subjective or psychological point of view. We saw the importance of the unconscious, the not-known as contrasted with the known, and the functional, creative effect of this tension. In the pathological basis of the love-struck archeologist we saw Jung's emphasis on the particularity of fantasy image and its longing beyond referents in the real world. We noted his work on psychopathological syndromes and mechanisms and the ways he differentiates these from, yet sees them of the same in origin as, creative states.

Obviously psychopathology was a fertile ground in the genesis of Jung's psychological ideas and methods. In its capacity as generative potential, the question as to what psychopathology is matters less than what can be done with it. Though there is no dearth of descriptions of the qualities that accompany pathological states—stereotypy, superficiality, egocentricity, dissociation, etc.—none of these qualities necessarily *determines* what is pathological. The significance of these is determined after the fact. Any of these components may be seen, given proper circumstances, in "normal" states as well, so that what comes to be called "pathological" depends on a series of evaluative judgments on the part of the diagnostician.

From the point of view of psychological making, this relativity is of no real concern, since for a psychopoiesis what is essential is not what a thing is, its reality (*Realität*), but its effect (*Wirklichkeit*), and definitions of what pathology is or is not of less import than what can be done with the assumption.[50] By viewing cer-

---

50. Cf. Chapter Six, note 35.

tain behaviors as defensive, compromising or delusional, the clinician assumes the criteria for a crafting that is qualitatively better. In evaluating psychopathology for its inadequacies, a differentiated view toward betterment is already implied. From this perspective, psychopathology may be seen as the *prima materia*, the basic material, from which psychological making proceeds. The pragmaticism implied by this view makes for a psychopoetics of diagnosis and treatment based wholly on evaluations that are essential for the making of psychology's therapeutic activities. Values, not facts, makings not science, form the basis of the psychotherapeutic discipline.

CHAPTER NINE

The Making of Therapeutic Treatment:
Notes to the Clinician

W e have seen psychopathology as a form of making determined to be inferior from a diagnostic point of view. The way a psychological situation is diagnosed— what is considered pathological and how this is determined— contains implications for treatment. In Chapter Seven we spoke of interpretation as a secondary making after the original dream-making. Similarly, therapeutic treatment may be taken as a secondary making after pathological making. In order to approach the question of therapeutic treatment, we ought consider some further issues regarding the context, structure and movement of psychopathology. As a focus for these considerations, let us again return to the pathological archeologist, since we are familiar with this case and it provides sufficient material from which we can see a pathological patterning and its dynamic.

We turn first to the question of context. Psychopathology is diagnosed as such within the context of a larger image. It is important to see what that context is in order to be aware of the terms of the diagnosis and the assumptions in the treatment. A context that is too narrow—e.g., a single situation, a symptom, a dream, even a series of dreams—lacks the scope necessary to show the interrelationships of a diagnostic picture.

For instance, the archeologist's situation before the outbreak of his illness was described by Jung as the situation of a scholar dedicated to his work, withdrawn from the world and buried in his books, engaged at the same time in producing important contributions for his field. He lived in secret fantasies revolving around a woman he had once known. His scholarly efforts were not to forget her "but to work for her in his thoughts."[1]

On the basis of this description one might imagine the situation as somewhat odd, perhaps lonely. The archeologist is probably an eccentric fellow. But the situation is not, given this context, pathological. There is no disturbing symptom and no evidence of an inferior making. Quite the contrary, the productions of this man, his scholarly work, are described as outstanding. What is simply peculiar, his isolated habits and interior fantasy life, is not within the context of this image pathological. For the diagnosis of pathology the clinician needs a broader (or in this case perhaps a more detailed) image.

But with the appearance of the symptom, the context alters. In this case the change is paralleled with a change in geographical situation; taking a holiday tour, the patient travels to the town of B.

> He walked a great deal in the environs of the town. The few acquaintances he had there found him strange, taciturn, and nervous. After a rather long walk he seemed very tired, and remarked that he did not feel very well. He then talked of getting himself hypnotized, as he felt nervously run down. On top of this he fell physically ill with inflammation of the lungs. Soon afterwards a peculiar state of excitement supervened, which rapidly passed over into frenzy. He was brought to the asylum, where for weeks he remained in an extremely excited state. He was completely deranged, did not know where he was, spoke in broken sentences which no one could understand. Often he was so excited and aggressive hat it took several attendants to hold him down.[2]

The symptoms presaging the breakdown appear first as the subject's nervousness, tiredness, physical illness, and then an

---

1. *CW*3: 350.
2. *CW*3: 342.

excitement which, as the disease progresses, devolves into states of frenzy, disorientation, and derangement.

The appearance of these symptoms shifts the context of the psychological situation and hence the point from which interpretation and treatment are oriented. The symptom is now the central focus, enough that other contexts (the subject's self-containment in his study) are seen in this light. But what is a symptom, or what makes a symptom symptomatic?

A symptom becomes symptomatic to the degree that it contrasts with an image of states considered normal or usual. In Chapter Three we mentioned the importance of contrast to a psychological aesthetics. The dynamic effect of contrast is crucial in pulling toward the foreground what is to be considered symptomatic or pathological. In this sense the symptomatic may be defined as that which disturbs another image, which disturbance is characterized by suffering. This suffering may be explicit, as w en a patient is aware of it; or it may be implicit, as when others are aware of it whether or not the patient feels it as suffering.

This definition of the symptom is appropriate to a psychopoetic mode of treatment. By relativizing the symptom as a contrast, the practitioner must be aware of the background against which the symptom is being viewed. And by keeping it relational, he need not make it coincide with general or collective judgments regarding what is symptomatic. Nervousness or the desire to be hypnotized may or may not be symptomatic, depending on the term of contrast. If a person who is generally seen as volatile appears suddenly calm and reasonable, this abrupt shift might be inferred as symptomatic, as might a shift from calm to volatility.

Because symptoms break with what has been the usual or normal state of affairs they point toward new contexts, which require new psychological makings. From this point of view, the symptom determines the context (rather than the context the symptom). The symptom takes our patient to the town B. and his consequent breakdown. It is not that the breakdown occurred because the patient was in town B., but that the need for a breakdown of the usual (his self-enclosed environment) created his trip to B. If we regard the needs of the psyche's making as primary, then the situations the psyche creates may be taken as necessary to that making. The psyche determines the situation.

A few years after his first breakdown, the patient once again returns to town B. and again suffers a breakdown, this time more seriously in that his symptoms include bizarre posturings and delusions. In answer to the obvious question concerning the reason for the patient's returning to the scene of his breakdown, let us hypothesize that he needs to break down, i.e., to break with previous patterns. Jung speaks of symptoms as intentional, by which he means that they possess a purpose, a telos. Symptoms are not simply reactive to situations, but create situations in keeping with their purposes.

We might say that, in its processes of making, the psyche produces symptoms to disrupt previous patterns so that new patternings can be created. The insistence of this destructive-constructive dynamic is such that symptoms will continue to repeat themselves until a new making of one sort or another results, or until the grounds of the situation shift.

Since the nature of the new making is unknown, symptoms appear contingent, blank, unintelligible (why does the patient return to the town of his suffering?) or bizarre (his posturing and his disordered talk make no immediate sense). Symptoms are unintelligible, bizarre and unaccountable because one does not comprehend the terms of the new making that is being urged. The destruction is clear, but that there is something to be gained from the destruction is less apparent. The reason for this obscurity is partly that symptoms in their teleological aspect are symbolic. They speak indirectly and by means of condensed, alogical conundrums, which generally appear as behavioral or bodily enactments. Also these condensations are not simply purposive and positive. They are also sufficiently conservative that once established they resist movement.

When the symptom settles in, it moves from its sense as a signal, a chance falling together (*symptoma*), to what may be more properly regarded as a pathological state, which as such resists making. These two aspects of the symptom, its symbolic urge toward making and its compromised self-containment, exist together. Hence therapeutic treatment involves breaking up the self-containment and furthering the urge toward new making.

In the previous chapter we spoke of pathology as an inferior making, a superficial solution. As the psyche breaks down, deconstructing its previous patterns of orientation and usual habits of thought, new makings take place. The shortest route for these new makings—i.e., if not slowed or deepened or worked through—is the condensation of a pathological compromise. One way this may be seen in the case of our patient is in his short-circuited "acting out." According to an authoritative definition, acting out refers to "manifesting the purposive behavior appropriate to an older situation in a new situation which symbolically represents it."[3] Translated into our terms, acting out may be regarded as the substitution of a prior pattern of making for the new making that is required. When these substitutions are acted out, they appear inappropriate, i.e., dissonant in the contexts in which they are enacted. The patient's violence with his attendants was his attempt to enact the psychic situation in terms more primitive and stereotypic than the situation called for. But these primitive enactments nonetheless symbolized it, in the sense that there was a psychic struggle going on, which *was* like the clashing of two

---

3. Horace B. and Ava C. English, *A Comprehensive Dictionary of Psychological and Psychoanalytical Terms* (New York: David McKay, 1958).

opposing forces. By identifying with one of these forces and viewing its counter as outside himself, the patient was able to enact
the psyche's processes in projected form. This drama, despite its
violence, remains superficial (i.e., pathological) insofar as its enemies remain exteriorized as hospital attendants. In this form they
are outside the possibilities of a resolution that could affect the
psychic situation as a whole, transmuting each of its parts. Rather
the situation was such that the episode came and went, leaving its
terms much the same as before.

Delusions are also inferior makings. The patient believed
himself an inspired poet, singer, composer, orator, and a physical specimen of great beauty. From an aesthetic point of view
these notions are delusional not because they are untrue or
unreal—psychologically they *are* real—but because they are held
in delusional ways. When an idea is held delusionally, its tone
is rigid, brittle, exclusive, without flexibility. While in his enactments, the patient was wholly identified with them. There was for
him no irony, reflection, distance, or the impersonality necessary
for craft. Rather than crafting his enactions through and among
their various tensions, the patient collapsed these tensions into
the rigid encompassment of a belief system. This rigidification,
by excluding the subtleties of contrast, tension, and ferro, obviated the possibility of more interesting psychological makings.

More interesting makings need not, however, depart from the
symptoms. To the contrary, if symptoms express psychic values
and the necessity of a new making with these values, then our
patient's symptoms—all of which involved the value of aesthetic
beauty and achievement—point toward their cure. The making
implied by these symptoms, the values they expressed, albeit
bizarrely, was essentially what the psyche was about.

The symptoms are the poetic plan, which, if it is to be fully
actualized, must be carried out along the lines of, in ways

mimetic with, the original makings of the symptoms. In this way cure does not depart from symptoms but deepens by rendering them more effectively. This does not mean of course that the patient ought literally to become a poet, orator, etc., but that the values symbolized by these roles have to be engaged and worked through in a manner that shapes them psychologically without losing their value.

According to Jung, the reverse happened. When the patient was discharged from his first hospitalization he returned to his usual life in a more exaggeratedly isolated way than before. "Gradually he got the reputation of being a dried-up misanthrope, with no feeling for the beauty of life."[4] The values expressed by the patient's symptoms in the context of town B. were denied and repressed in his return to the former context of his study.

Elsewhere Jung refers to this mode of movement as a "regressive restoration of the persona."[5] The regression shows as the attempt to return to a previous context as if no new making had occurred. Since the psychological context has changed in the interim, return is not possible without a reworking of it in terms of what has occurred. "Normality" becomes a regression when it does not take account of the psyche's symptoms, or of what has been effected by the psyche's breakdown.

In Chapter Five we maintained that the figure behind the patient's symptoms, the beloved woman for whom he longed, was a form of what Jung calls the anima, and as such she was an imaginal figure pertaining to imaginal needs. From this point of view the patient's longing was for a particular quality of the imagination, a quality that exists between realms and beyond the actuality of literal fulfillment. For this reason it is unlikely that literal

---

4. *CW*3: 342.

5. *CW*7: 254–59, 471–75.

union with the woman of his memories could ever have occurred. Nor should it have.

The nature of his longing is manifested by the circumstances of its appearance. His desires fixed themselves on an object patently unattainable. At the time of his relation with the actual woman, the patient did not pursue the involvement because of his shyness. Later he let it lapse because he had heard she was married. If we regard these reasons, given by the patient in justifying his lack of literal involvement, from a purposive point of view, we may grasp this lack as aiding a construction of another sort-one which values longing without consummation. As we recall in the patient's fantasy (Chapter Seven), the moment of aesthetic interest involved not a final union but a focus on the moment of drawing near.

The quality of these circumstances fits the nature of anima as Jung describes it. For Jung the anima cannot be achieved or psychologically compassed, since her value, as with Jung's dove-girl in Chapter One, is to connect beyond what is actual. As prototypical of the imagination in general, she is the unattainable, an aesthetic yearning apart from the possibility of literal attainment. Thus considered, what our patient most essentially yearns for is an imaginal quality like the one inspired by the unattainable lady of his fantasies. She is the *causa finalis* of his struggles. His delusional enactments are performed for her.

While he is in hospital, containment is provided for these enactments. On his return home, however, there is a reconstitution no longer allowing this expression. Though we are told he continues to fantasize about his beloved, something in the situation is amiss, as evidenced by the fact that he must again return to B. in order to break down and enact his delusional renderings. It is as if the making required by his psyche cannot occur within the context of his usual life. But what is his usual life? Following Jung we can only suppose that the structure of our patient's life is such that his fantasies exist in an interior realm isolated from surrounding contingencies. In this self-containment he became increasingly withdrawn from the context within which he was living.

We have spoken of the realm of anima as a place between realities such that it participates in both interior and exterior worlds. As imaginally based, the anima defies rigid boundaries and demarcations, since these curtail imaginative movements and possibilities of making.

From this point of view, our patient's problem may be seen as in part a structural one. The overdetermination of boundaries between his inner world of fantasy and outer world of engagement and action inhibits the possibility of movement between these realms. Thus he was either sequestered in his study or wildly active (in his posturing and aggressive behavior). Town B. was a potent context for the solution of this problem since both worlds—inner and outer, fantasy and actuality—met there. The result was a collocation of forces necessary to the required imaginal making but for which the patient was unprepared, had not developed the means for handling.

Overdetermined boundaries are like thick outlines in a painting. Sometimes these work, in which case they help to express what the painting is about and so further the aesthetic purpose of the painting. But the purpose of our archeologist's painting (if we may so imagine it) as expressed through his anima longings and symptoms, does not lend itself to (rather is disturbed by) such divisions. This is particularly the case since the anima, as we have seen, tends generally toward dissolution of boundaries rather than their reification.

Given these understandings of our case, how would we go about treatment? We spoke above of the role of symptoms in determining the context of treatment. The symptoms before and during the patient's first internment—disorientation, confused ideas, and aggression—denote a context in which breakdown is necessary, since the symptoms themselves are breaking with established patterns. At this point in treatment, support must be given—not in order to stop this process but to create conditions making possible its continuance. The hospital (where abnormality is the norm) provides this kind of containment, as does a therapeutic attitude that values the psyche's deconstruction. But valuing is not enough, for unless these processes are given form through images or other mimetic means, they will tend to cohere into delusional patterns.

The therapeutic task, its making, has to do with exploring these processes by bringing forth its movements and patterns. The means of exploration are mimetic, like the psyche's processes, and formative in that they give definition to them. We may remember Jung's techniques in dealing with his own madness. By giving his imaginal figures names, discerning their characteristics, drawing them, speaking with them, building his constructions of mud and stone, Jung-actively worked with the psyche's makings. This activity provided shape and tangibility even to the psyche's dispersal so it could be felt and seen through the senses. Thus the activity became an aisthesis in which the psyche's processes were mirrored and its attempts at origination aided. Since, as we have maintained, the psyche is basically a maker, it will indeed make, whether this occurs as the catastrophism of pathology or the slower, more attentive making of craft.

Also important in the craft of treatment is a consideration of the psyche's structures and how these structures are involved in support of the symptomatic processes. We have seen the difficulty with the boundaries demarking the patient's interior from his exterior life. This rigidity worked counter to the psyche's makings, creating of them exaggerated over-enactments. So another intention of therapeutic treatment is to soften and encourage the flexibility of this line. The practitioner might do this in various ways. Most simply, he or she may encourage imaginal, sensuous qualities in every manner of manifestation—whether in the patient's interior fantasy life or as outer fascinations or interests. If conceived interiorly, the qualities would be related exteriorly; if exteriorly then also interiorly, so the sense of reverberation across realms becomes evident and divisions less important.

The treatment here proposed is distinct from current therapies based (like Jung's scientific stance) on an assumption of internal/external divisions. A therapy founded on making is not concerned with what reality is—whether inner or outer or both—but with how and to what effect it allows of being worked. Underlying ontologies and structures matter only to the extent that these affect what is accomplished in the making. Psychopathology provides the contrasts by which these makings can be evaluated. That is to say, by assuming what is generally called the psychopathological to be makings of an inadequate sort, makings that imperfectly express the psyche's possibilities, we provide a means of contrast that prefers to ontologies or states of being the immediacies of a making process. In Chapter Three we discussed the role of negation in the underlying aesthetics of depth psychology, seeing it as a field of tensions and contrasts by means of which psychological awarenesses occur. The negativism implied in regarding psychopathology as an inferior form of making is therefore not to be taken literally—it claims no ontological status—but may be more appropriately regarded as a tool, a means by which the making of psychotherapy proceeds.

This attitude to the psyche's making leads to implications different from those currently assumed in therapeutic treatment.

Since most therapies are based on an internal/external division and an assumption of reality as external, they will maintain that the pathology of our patient derives from an overemphasis on fantasy which then results in loss of contact with reality. Given these assumptions, treatment would encourage the patient to give up his fantasies and to focus more realistically on issues relating to external reality.

Treatment from this point of view is not without therapeutic effect. It has the aesthetic advantage of simplicity and direct-ness, in that it works from the very divisions the patient has set up, and reverses those values. The interior life the patient indulges is in this approach suppressed and his feel for exterior life encouraged. Hence through simple reversal a psychic econ-omy is encouraged which may then be worked with fairly directly. Whereas this mode of treatment takes advantage of the patient's basic constructs, it neglects the more idiosyncratic or intimate psychic processes.

A psychopoetic treatment would focus on the particularities of these makings. By assuming the psyche to be essentially a pro-cess of making and these makings by definition originary, that is to say more basic than assumptions about them, treatment would look to each particular making to discern its generating intentionality. If the symptom, for instance, values poetry, ora-torical accomplishment or physical beauty, then these contents would be considered important. Whether the patient imagines himself Jesus, Nietzsche or a poet will create differences in the associative field, entailing different considerations for therapeu-tic treatment.

In addition to content the form of the disorder is also impor-tant. Delusions of reference, delusions of meaning, delusions of identity, quite apart from their particular contents, have differ-ent formal implications as well. Whereas delusions of reference concern the manner in which relations between the subject and his world are construed, delusions of meaning focus on significances within things. Delusions of identity concern the subject himself. The delusions of grandeur evidenced by our patient are a form of identity disorder. In his case the delusion becomes self-incorporated, "swallowed" so that it appears as an inflated self-identity. The appearance of these and other forms in pathology gives us clues to the psyche's intentionality. If reference is being stressed, the therapy would concern itself with reference between the subject and his world. If meaning, questions of meaning or meaninglessness would become an issue, and so with grandeur in its implications for self-identity.

From a psychopoetic point of view, the particular forms and contents of pathological syndromes point toward their cures. They give the ground plan, so to speak, by which new makings in the form of psychological treatment proceed. Psychic manifestations are never "wrong," though they may be incomplete or rendering inadequately what they are about. A psychopoetic approach assumes the making processes of the psyche to be unifying, richly complex interrelationships.

Of the various ways this interrelational complexity gets distorted through pathology, two underlying means appear generally relevant. These are identification and splitting. By identification we refer to the subject's tendency to ego-identify with one or another aspect of a psychic movement or situation. In identifying with one aspect of an image process, the ego caricatures and simplifies the aesthetic possibilities of the situation. This identification can occur along moral lines, as though the subject were all good or all bad. It may occur in terms of power, as though the subject were in control and all powerful, or conversely, with no control and victimized. It could appear in terms of psychological functions, as if the subject is only intellectual (all mind and no body), or only physical, as if the subject is a creature of habit and appetite. Whatever the particular form and content of the identification the result is a splitting of psychological aspects so that some are denied, projected or simply repressed.

Pathological simplification denies the potential richness and depth of psychological making. The primordial image Jung posits as forming the basis of psychic life is a purposefully complex, richly ambiguous and mysterious notion. In working from an awareness of this and its basis in *esse in anima,* psychological treatment attempts to reclaim and rework the psyche's potential. Thus the making that treatment intends, its psychopoiesis, is to aid and further engender the psyche's making processes.

CHAPTER TEN

Concluding Reflections

My attempt has been to gather principles for a psycho-poetic approach to interpretation and treatment from Jung's early work in psychiatry. Since this endeavor has itself been a form of making, I conclude by offering a reflection on what I have been about and the method entailed.

The *esse in anima* guiding this procedure appeared in Jung's personal breakdown. During this period of pathological conflict and disorientation, Jung disavowed *the aesthetic lady* who informed him that his activities were art. Also there appeared the dove-girl in his dream (anima-like in her duplicity as human and spirit), the sensuous Salome and her snake (of whom Jung was distinctly suspicious), and Ka the craftsman, who obscured Philemon (the halcyon spirit with which Jung identified meaning).

In addition to these figures, my approach looked to Jung's symptomatic behaviors. Having lost the conceptual framework of what he was about professionally, Jung listened without judgment to his patients' dreams and reports. Unable to locate causal explanations for his difficulties, he resorted to makings that were mimetic, repeating a boyhood passion for building with mud and stone.

I drew from this period in Jung's life an orientation for my psychopoetic. By focusing on Jung's personal pathology—a pathology that showed multiple imaginary figures—I grounded my approach in the context of the symptomatic, the unusual or abnormal. From this attention to pathology my psychopoetic perspective emerged.

The figures Salome, Ka, and *the aesthetic lady* whom Jung devalued, I revalued. These figures provided the unconscious movement that my mimetic procedure imitated. I followed the qualities that they represented. My orientation from the unknown in Jung's original construction unbalanced his renderings by means of the very contrasts he had given. His values—meaning (Philemon) versus beauty (Ka), theoretical interpretation versus immediate hearing, abstract system (the mandala) versus concrete making, wisdom (Elijah, Philemon) versus sensuousness (Salome, snake—were in this action reversed, so that Jung's background became for us foreground.

Despite this reversal of Jung's perspective and his emphasis, my method throughout participated mimetically with his contrasts and their terms. In this way the scientific and systematic devalued in our approach was nonetheless assumed through its negation. I never departed from Jung. Whereas Jung's rendering was more imaginative and less literal than the medical positivism he countered, mine was yet again less literal. In basing my view explicitly on the imaginal that was devalued in Jung's construction, his *appeared* as if more literal and mine less so. Yet in this movement I have followed Jung's own method of inventing literal positions against which more psychological constructions can be made. Essential to Jung's psychological procedure and to mine has been just this movement. In the course of this activity, perspectives have changed and values transformed and other constructions such as those in this dissertation appear. Even the principles I have offered deriving from Jung's *esse in anima*—contrast, movement, the unknown, along with the interpretive and therapeutic means associated with them—must themselves become subject to the very method of psychopoetic making that I have been attempting to exhibit. Only by regarding my own constructions as further possibilities for movement could I maintain a fruitfully imaginative psychology, which has been the one constant aim of this work.

www.ingramcontent.com/pod-product-compliance
Lightning Source LLC
Chambersburg PA
CBHW031433270326
41930CB00007B/692